FINDIN
THE
MUSIC INSIDE

Your inner algorithm to a more

meaningful life!

REYNOLDS

Finding the Music Inside

ISBN978-1-5272-5710-8

Contents

Introduction
Intro to my Flow

Your life has purpose.

Your story is important.

Your dreams count.

Your voice matters.

You were born to make an impact.

Author unknown

L ondon was my home, it understood me. Me and my boys could hang out, no worries. No knife crime, no post code beef, our only concern was the national front not each other. I always found comfort from seeing people like me, not colour but culture. I could move how I wanted, like a ghost. London has a music of its own, each area does. I was raised listening to the city music. cars, sirens, people playing music, the sound of chatter, it would serenade me to sleep. I miss my boys, the stages we rocked, the time on the road touring. The bonds we built and the people we met along the way. I was a part of something powerful. I will never get bored of imagining the perfect future, at the same time transforming my reality. I sometimes daydream, staring into what could be. Wondering how long it will take for me to restore and ignite my inner passion again. It was a dark time in my life that shook me into life. Even after so many years the pain is still vivid. I thought people were lying when they shared about how they felt. I'd heard it described before, how it was supposed to feel. How, the second they were gone, they took a part of you with them. However, nothing could've prepared me for losing my mum. She was my inspiration and that could be the reason why I wanted to find my music again. Imagine feeling the most important part of your life dissolve into a sea of nothing. I took it for granted that she would always be there.

Let me introduce myself, I am Basil Reynolds. I was the founding member of the pioneering Hip Hop group the London Rhyme Syndicate. Before you ask, I was emceeing in the nineteen eighties. This is my journey of discovery and journey of recovery, finding my music inside.

I sat in my small mentoring room with a heaviness in my heart. I wasn't making the difference I dreamed I would make. I felt trapped as I wasn't in my area of influence. I doodled rhymes and still found myself making up rhymes as I listened to music, deep down I knew something was missing. I reminisced about my time as an emcee in the pioneering days of UK hip hop. The look in my parent's eyes when I gave them a signed copy of my first single. At that time, I felt alive, my work at no point felt like work. I was truly living life. What happened to me, why had I drifted so far from what made me unique. Why was I now playing to the narrative of a system that labels me in a limiting way? Why was I playing it safe? I was making decisions based on the income I needed to earn. I denied my passion as the pressures of life encamped around me. My wellbeing didn't matter and so I thought. I sacrificed what I loved because I believed I was being responsible. We get told so many things, we are given so much advise so we can be what someone else wants us to be. We can either get busy making someone else a profit or get busy making that profit for yourself. The pressures of life can act like a virus attacking our wellbeing leaving us defenseless. Things we were immune from in the past we are now vulnerable too. I felt low, I felt I had nothing of value to contribute. These feelings of worthlessness have a way of keeping us in situations well below our worth. If you feel like nothing others will treat you that way. Einstein said a mind in motion stays in motion unless it's disturbed by an outside voice. My disruption came at the passing of my mother. She always believed in me and inspired me to be better than I was. It was then I remembered my music, my passion inside. I remembered the stages I graced and the venues I rocked. I had to dig deep as they had been buried beneath so much doubts and fears. I had become accustomed in believing the limiting beliefs that stripped me of my truth. As soon as I focused on who I was my passion began to flow through me, my music was reawakened. I put pen to paper and wrote 'Dear hip hop.' I poured my heart out as I believed I needed to do more. Hip hop gave me a voice and a platform, I had stopped using mine.

You aren't hip hop, you're not even a pillar,

Your just a brick in fact not even a filler,

You're the link from the greats but you're not one,

Your content betrays on every album,

All the p (pennies) in the world will never hide one,

Rich or poor don't matter still a fake one,

Not a great one I save that for the pioneers,

Open up your ears this philosophy you fear,

Skilled in verse or just perverse I'll let you decide,

Hip hop culture from you I'm never gonna hide,

Catchy hooks with irrelevant rhymes,

Irreverent times, combine on every line,

It's not a joke, you're on dope, and I quote its broke,

Bring that weak shit over here and we know who's

getting choked,

From the kings and the queens, hoods and now fiends,

Remember where we've been the type shit we've seen,

I never wrote for the glory it's to gory,

From the killing of Emmett Till we replay the same

story,

Getting beat on the streets, shot on the streets,

Choked on the streets while you jump on the beat,

Youth packing heat on the block getting volatile,

We seem to fit a negative profile,

I think we love a negative profile,

We love the swag and the ice (Jewellery) as we act wild,

We send a message to the next generation,

We don't care about your extermination,

How long can we hide behind the music,

They confuse it with authentic true shit,

Look back and see where we came from,

While they're murdering out youth for no reason,

What you're saying really don't mean none,

Ain't nothing changed we still fighting for our

freedom,

Now you're wealthy you've forgotten what it's all about,

Shove your wealth in the faces of the down and out,

There the ones who bought your first mixtape,

They identified with you now they can't relate,

Now it's all about the image and the prestige,

What you drive what you wear like a big cheese,

Like a big weave, air brush to look plush,

No rush, so many bodies in the crush,

In every verse we hear the syntax of a racist,

The basis your trying to reclaim it,

It was never ours to use, so I refuse,

It was the last thing some brothers heard before the noose,

I'll never choose to lose while I'm still awake,

We know the snakes and the dialogue prone to hate,

Making threats licking shots from the tech 9,

Shooting your peeps you must be on the Feds side,

Dear hip hop we owe you an apology,

The whole scene embraces the anomaly,

Old school psychology, is where I'm taking you

Where from the block the one you never passed through,

But it really doesn't matter,

We all know the difference between an Emcee and a

rapper,

I'd love to sit down and explain it,

I hope this type of joint will always makes your playlist.

It was at this point I had an epiphany, I was born to be on stage, to make difference. The truth hit me; I have a passion to see others overcome the limited beliefs they are facing. This wasn't a new concept for me.

Hip hop is one of the few cultures that celebrated the inner city. I truly embraced the fact that it celebrated me, people that looked like me, dressed like me and spoke like me. The confidence I drew from this gave me the energy to believe in myself. This is due in part to hip hop's birthplace, the South Bronx of New York City. In Essence, hip hop embodies the feelings of inner-city youth, and the music and art reflect the harsh realities of inner-city life. The appreciation for such an underappreciated environment become a symbol of celebration as did the pioneering leaders of the artform. This appreciation can in some part be explained by the study of aesthetics. The definition of aesthetic is being interested in how something looks and feels.

Aesthetics is the branch of philosophy that focuses on the nature of beauty, how we look at the arts and the responses they produce. From desolate surroundings the culture of Hip-Hop was born. Young men and women, making the best of a terrible situation, they proved to be fertile soil. Young people left to rot in the ghetto, developed a powerful voice, that reached across the Atlantic. It was the Blues of the new working classes.

"The thing about hip-hop is that it's from the underground, ideas from the underbelly, from people who have mostly been locked out, who have not been recognized."

Russell Simmons, co-founder of Def Jam Recordings

Chuck D of Public Enemy proclaimed hip-hop as the "Black CNN," and the original gangsta rappers NWA declared, "it's not about a salary it's all about reality." That said, hip-hop has always been a way of attaining and distributing street news. That has never changed. The term news reflects both positive and negative stories, not just a one-sided narrative. We can never stop bearing witness. Ahmir Khalib Thompson, known professionally as Questlove, is an American musician and music journalist. He was the drummer and joint front man for the Grammy Award-winning band The Roots. Quest love wrote on Instagram, "I urge and challenge musicians and artists alike to push themselves to be a voice of the times that we live in.

This has led me to become a speaker, author and coach who specialises in seeing people find their music inside. To see limited beliefs broken in people's lives. To see everyone, do that one thing they were born to do. I have a strong inner motivation to influence people and their circumstances. The stresses and pressures of everyday work and life can drown out your inner music, I am here to help you to listen and start to dance again. Just like we did as children. When we live as we were created to be, we show how unique and powerful we are. That still small quiet voice inside is and has always reminded us of our value. To bring something out of nothing brings us all closer to our ideals than many of us appreciates. It could be a song, a rhyme, an idea, as we search within and bring our dreams into the real world. Our creative identity gives us the foundation to overcome limiting beliefs. As we overcome them our collective lights will shine brighter.

I started to write, this time it was not in a rhyme, but I began documenting my journey and the processes I experienced as I was reawakened. I found my music inside, then I let it go and now I was returning to my own dance. I could hear my music again. My mind aligned in the right way as I felt a similar balance to what I experienced when I was performing. It felt powerful and empowering as I chose to be who I was made to be. Talent is everywhere, but opportunity is not. In some instances, you must create the chances to be the person you are supposed to be. Our music inside gives a voice to our dreams and makes the invisible visible. My rap poetry has always been a part of my journey and awakening, so I have placed within each chapter a dose of rhyme. I hope this book will set your life in motion. Everyone has got that one thing they were born to do, your music inside that enables you to have a more meaningful life. I hope this story will inspire you to begin your own journey to find your music inside so you can achieve your best in life.

"The two most important days in your life are the day you are born
and the day you find out why."
Mark Twain

Chapter 1
I am here

*"Everyone has been made for some particular work and
the desire for that work has been put in every heart."*
Jalaluddin Rumi

The Echoes street chart was the go-to chart for urban hip hop music in the eighties. That's where you could find the latest hip hop songs that were blowing up. I rushed out to buy the paper as I had just released my first single, 'Hard to the Core', with my group, the London Rhyme Syndicate. I frantically searched through the paper until I found the street charts. Number one was Public Enemy, number two was Jewel T, I Like It Loud. Number three was Mantronix, number four was the

1

Jungle Brothers, and number five, the London Rhyme Syndicate, Hard to the Core. We made it! I was so excited, I sprinted to the nearest phone box to tell my mum the great news. Below us, there were some illustrious names – pioneers in hip hop. Eric B and Rakim, Salt 'N' Pepa, Ultramagnetic MC's, Kool Moe Dee, Big Daddy Kane, Easy E, KRS One and Scott La Rock, Kurtis Blow and Dougie Fresh. This piece was written in the NME music paper on the release of our single:

"Despite what a lot of people may say, British hip hop will never seriously challenge the U.S version. It just doesn't have the same culture that produces the same hard edge to the music. The media can effortlessly support it and plug it, but it wasn't B-Boys who bought the Derek B album that's for sure.

This however is B-Boy and it is British. The London Rhyme Syndicate have sussed What the British are best at doing, utilising the best records hot on the club scene over here and sticking them on their own records. A lively, funky record that is bound to shift a few copies in the city."

This was the challenge I was facing. They limited our experience and ability to connect with our generation. They also denied the very culture we had been living. Fresh out of the riots and we were still having to fight for our voices to be heard. But something inside me had changed. This was my music inside, this gave my life purpose and meaning. It doesn't matter how old you are or what you have been through. It doesn't matter if you have failed a thousand times and you want to throw in the towel, we face the inner struggle against self-limiting beliefs. I thought it wasn't possible, I couldn't do it, I wasn't good enough. I repeated what my inner world was reflecting.

Everyone wants to tell you what to do and what's good for

you.

They don't want you to find your own answers, they want

you to believe theirs.

Socrates

When I listened to rap music, the self-confidence oozed through me. I started to believe in my abilities and my purpose became clear. I was going to make hip hop music and perform on the biggest stages. I visualized my way out of the dark hole of doubt, I was going to be the type of individual who would always get back up. I knew that if I stayed in the game, I would get there in the end. If you stay in the game, you will have the opportunity to discover your passion and play your music. Maybe you found your music long ago but the pressures of life have snuffed out your candle. There is still hope, there is still time, it doesn't matter what age you are, you can find and play your music inside.

Let silent words be heard alliteration understood,

Did things I never thought I would and never over

stood,

I went through things I never would and never should

was good,

From any hood we are the outlaws seen not Robin

Hood,

My rhyme vernacular grammatical spectacular,

It's how we came, using skills at will to massacre,

I challenge yer, the sound of silence our reliance to

violence,

And our compliance gives license, that's why we are

dropping this science,

Dichotic verses hypnotise, its hypnotic,

Like a tonic you take it's so ironic,

Psychotic psychosis, the iconic they know this,

I'm dipping in and dipping out, I realise in small doses,

Responsibility is mine to make that small-time shine,

So many focus on their self to toe the line is a crime,

So rewind don't be blind I'm taking this to the floor,

> *War was declared in the beginning and it can't be*
> *ignored,*
> *We react then scatter, every life it matters,*
> *Most talk will flatter, the innocent on the platter,*
> *Like a prophet I deposit my truth in the socket,*
> *Don't knock it for profit they fill their pockets and*
> *wallets,*
> *With gossip they mock it, with knowledge we stop it,*
> *The psychotic biopic, real life and I drop it,*
> *Words of silence are so violent when there not*
> *understood,*
> *We can't be silent but defiant if we want to do good.*

My brother Arnold decided the time was right to introduce me to the new underground craze. He played Kurtis Blow the Breaks. He cued up the song and my eardrums exploded like they had heard something for the first time; they came alive and sparked emotions that music had left untouched. The beat did something inside of me, I had no explanation,

I just kept playing the song on repeat. The wordplay transformed popular music, he wasn't singing, this brother rapped. It connected with me. Hearing the song for the first time compared to riding a roller coaster for the first time. The pounding rhythm, no compromise in style, the hard-hitting poetry appealed to me. This music was in your face, unapologetic, just loud and proud. As the moon signaled the night, I knew I wanted to do this.

On the flip side each record had an instrumental, my playground and workshop rolled into one. I loved bass and hip hop was unrepentant in its use. Radical, edgy and rebellious at the same time. When 'Rockbox' landed from Run DMC I couldn't get enough, stereotypes were being blown away, this music is hardcore. It didn't follow the traditional music formats, it created new ones. I listened to music led by the melody, and the rhythm supported the vocals. But hip hop the rhythm led with the melody supporting. I played it loud as I wanted to feel I was inside the song. I could tell from my parents' facial expressions that they didn't share my enthusiasm for hip hop. They soon tired of telling me to turn it down. They said the ceiling sounded like it was coming down, all they could hear was the boom boom boom of the bass drum, that's why some called it boom bap music. Music is life that's why our hearts have beats.

I was never the best emcee, I didn't have to be, I had a place and a story to tell. It elevated me, gave me a platform, that's what music can do. it's about the emotions that carry with you through every note.

My music inside was the only part of me that ever kept me sane. You would always see me with my headphones and a pen and pad. My dreams would never be the same. Music brought me out of myself and launched me into great experiences that I will never forget.

I think a number of the leaders are, whether you like it or not, in the hip-hop generation. And when they understand enough, they'll do wonders. I count on them.

Maya Angelou

Hip hop culture, my culture my rebellion, reclaimed the public spaces to our spaces. Sometimes through sound, sound systems pumping out the latest songs. At other times through the writing and images on walls and trains. Whenever I saw it, I knew this is my spot, I belong here. The culture of Hip Hop founded with four elements, the DJ, the Emcee, the Graffiti artist and the Break Boys. These values sustained the movement and provided it with the platform for growth. We each need to have values and to live by them. Before emcees were artists, DJ's were the original acts that attracted crowds to the block parties and clubs. A legendary DJ who called himself Grand Wizard Theodore made a significant discovery while practicing in his bedroom. Theodore's mum interrupted him causing his hand to stop the record and produce a sound now known as scratching. Around the same time, Grandmaster Flash developed his theory that allowed him full control over the turntable with a precision in his mixing that was completely unrivaled in the early days, he called it the quick mix. When you find your music and begin to let it play, it doesn't take long for self-limiting beliefs to confront you. Flash received criticism because his new style had him putting his hands all over the records, potentially damaging or dirtying the needles and record discs.

These DJ's quickly became celebrities and artists in their own right. Now the same song played by different DJ's had the flexibility to sound different depending on the DJ playing it. Over time the DJ was supported by an MC's and as they began to get more creative in their methods of pumping the crowd up, they eventually become part of the show. Rap only refers to the vocal style and does not represent the philosophy. I like how KRS-One puts it best, "Rap is something you do, Hip Hop is something you live." Hip Hop is about so much more than rapping, but this type of vocal performance is an essential piece of Hip-Hop culture and the history behind it goes so much deeper.

The art of emceeing stems from the practice of oral history and oral tradition, which can be dated back to a concept that was founded in Western Africa called nommo. As a concept in philosophy, nommo is the power of words to shape reality, act upon objects and give life to ideas. This idea paved the way for traveling griots to rise in importance for African tribal communities. Griots cataloged mass amounts of knowledge and history in their minds to share it with people who had no other way of learning about places and ideas from outside of their immediate surroundings. Centuries later, rhyme and verbal teaching remained as an aid to both spread and preserve ideas. The term and concept of an emcee, the

MC. This acronym stands for Master of Ceremonies and later "move the crowd," an alliteration created by Rakim for his 1987 song of the same name.

DJ Kool Herc was the first to sample drum loops or "breaks" by using a double disc turntable. This kept the people in the crowd dancing, as it was a way to perpetuate the most rhythmic part of the music. This is also how B-Boys or Break Boys earned their name, by creating a new style of dance to match Herc's pioneering music. B-Boying was used by the different crews to settle conflicts.

Graffiti first came to public attention in the late 1960s, mostly in New York City. It came out of a movement for Black and Hispanic identity and empowerment. In the 1970s and 80s it became part of the hip-hop style. The tag was a stylized logo that allowed an artist to paint subway cars yet remain anonymous. Graffiti writers used tags to compete for public space and attention.

Through hip hop and the way these cultural pioneers used their record collection pushed me to dig deeper. My parents record collection got my attention. I listened intently for the drum breakdowns and instrumental sections in all their records. Matching particular sections of James Brown songs to the hip hop songs I was listening too.

My rap style was initially influenced by the rappers from New York, but my flow developed into my own voice. It was similar to reggae DJ's, no matter where they were from sounded Jamaican, as that was the epicenter for the music. Over time we were on the journey of being ourselves and showing who we were on vinyl. It soon became about representing our thing and using our experience to represent our culture. My passion had been awakened, when DJ Kool Herc emerged in 1974 as a social storyteller over beats, he influenced the music of Kurtis Blow, Grandmaster Flash and the Sugar Hill Gang and me.

British hip hop was now a thing and we had our own pioneers. The heartbeat of the scene was around Covent Garden and Leicester Square. From nothing to something our hip-hop culture was strong, thanks to the whole diversity of cultural skills that were on display. Identity is the launchpad for destiny. We excelled in graffiti, breaking, popping and locking, but this was only part of our story. Guys were hustling trying to fulfill their dreams, finding their music inside. We had to be resilient as we faced prejudice from those who would eventually benefit from the scene. Some West end clubs had a no blacks door policy so we would often rush the back doors of the clubs to hear the music we loved. From the days of Electro, from Spats to Cinderella Rockefella's we witnessed the rise of true Kings and Queens. I would make my pilgrimage to Charing Cross tube station to watch the New York craze in London style. I couldn't get enough of this new sound, new dance and new art. It was B-Boys popping and locking, the floor work was unreal, it defied traditional dances that were around at the time. I didn't know many of the guys, but it didn't matter, I loved the vibe. I loved the style and unique identity being formed, I needed to be a part of it. Covent Garden was the place where the energy for the London scene was birthed. The ripple effect vibrated across London and beyond.

Hip-hop was created out of necessity. We needed to create some digitized things to help us understand what we were feeling.

Erykah Badu

Bluebirds records sold the freshest mixtapes out of the Bronx, New York. The UK was ripe for this new culture to take hold. This was happening at the same time as Margaret Thatcher became prime minister. Things were about to become dire for the inner cities and urban youth. This music soon became our escape, In Ladbroke Grove under the Westway you had the hall of fame for artists. I would ride my BMX down to Westway to view the urban gallery and watch the artists in action.

Soul and Funk were deeply embedded within our fabric, but in school it was mods and rockers, Punk was the music they chose to reflect their anger. Reggae and Dancehall from Jamaica was more relevant to me as I was the child of Jamaican heritage. I remember my dad telling me about the first Jamaican owned recording studio and record label in the UK, Planetone in Kilburn. The pride in his eyes spoke to my insecurities of making something of my life. This diverse cocktail of influences would be the foundation of us developing our own voice. The only way I can describe it is contagious, I remember it didn't take long before these sounds would be heard in the clubs, on the streets, in youth centres and in school yards. In a few short years we had developed and refined the culture and we were incorporating into our lives. I don't know how many times I was directed to look outside of myself to find my passion, when it was inside me just waiting to be put in motion.

Invictus

Out of the night that covers me,

Black as the Pit from pole to pole,

I thank whatever gods may be

For my unconquerable soul.

In the fell clutch of circumstance

I have not winced nor cried aloud.

Under the bludgeonings of chance

My head is bloody, but unbowed.

Beyond this place of wrath and tears

Looms but the Horror of the shade,

And yet the menace of the years

Finds, and shall find, me unafraid.

17

It matters not how strait the gate,

How charged with punishments the scroll.

I am the master of my fate:

I am the captain of my soul.

William Ernest Henley

Invictus, means unconquerable or undefeated in Latin, it is a poem by William Ernest Henley. The poem was written while Henley was in the hospital being treated for tuberculosis. He had the disease from a young age, and had his foot amputated shortly before he wrote the poem. The poem focuses on the human spirit and its ability to overcome adversity. It is a rallying cry for those who find themselves in dark and trying situations, who have to dig deep and fight for their lives. No piece of poetry better embodies the spirit of hip hop like this.

I would spend hours searching my analogue radio trying to find anything that resembled hip hop.

If it wasn't for pirate radio stations who knows if it would have blown up the way it did over here. Putting their freedom at risk to serve us the music we wanted to here. We couldn't get airplay on mainstream stations but thankfully the rise of the pirates, they gave us a platform to showcase our talents. They fed us the Music we loved and played the music we made. Many superstar DJ's were founded and grounded in the pirate radio space.

I knew what I wanted to be, and I could see it every time I closed my eyes. I knew what it would feel like, how the microphone would feel in my hand. I could see the crowd responding and making noise, I visualized all of it. I wanted with all my being for this dream to be real. Keeping it real was the ultimate claim for the successful hip-hop artist. It was the opposite of being called fake, that was seen as the ultimate disrespect. Being true to oneself and representing one's place and culture were vital aspects of keeping it real. One might also describe these qualities as your individuality. We have all been given unique gifts that define who we are, this is our music inside. It all starts by seeing things as they are not what I wished they were. Nothing faced can be changed and nothing changes unless it's faced. Dreams are birthed in the most unusual places. In a climate of poverty, the Bronx expressway forced the Bronx community into recession. In this climate young pioneers found their music inside and used it to mobilise a generation. Hip hop was born. We all have talents and gifts, and the world is a richer place when we walk in who we are made to be and shine our lights. We are taught to be safe and chase what is normal all the while ignoring how special we are. We are guided towards careers based on financial rewards. We don't take into consideration what truly aligns who we are with what we do. The focus seems to be more on what we do than who we are. I always say hip hop found me. The key to who we are is inside us. The very things we are passionate about are clues to the careers we are best served in. It is our duty, our duty to discover our music or I should say uncover it. For some of us it may be hidden under a barrage of negativity and limiting beliefs. We might be stuck in a cycle of behaviour. You may be asking; how can I start my journey? You start where all the great stories start by taking the first step.

"The mystery of human existence lies not in just staying alive, but in finding something to live for."

Fyodor Dostoyevsky

I always had something to say. My school report attested to this. But it was when I appeared on the Yo MTV Rap show, my music inside had the platform to shine beyond my expectations. My critics limited my gift as they couldn't see what I could see. I believe that our purpose in life is to discover our music inside. For many of us, we may hide our music inside under a barrage of negativity and limiting beliefs, but it is still there. On the cloudiest day, the sun is still shining behind the clouds.

You may find yourself in a cycle of behavior. It's time to flip the script. Flipping the script refers to turning the tables, doing the unexpected, or deviating from the norm. Hip-hop culture was established on the premise of flipping existing material in new and innovative ways. From break dancers repurposing discarded flooring to graffiti artists using subway cars and alleyways as canvases, representing hip-hop's philosophy of taking things and transforming things. These hip-hop pioneers flipped the script on how society viewed them. We were the new urban story tellers. for the first time we were packaged as brands and caused a revolution. They flipped the script and said something was bad meaning good. We often limit ourselves by deciding we can't do something before we even try. When we do that, we've stopped our growth and our path to success. This negative self-talk is a clear sign that you need to rewrite your script, flip the script. Our script affects what we do, where we go and how we approach life. A powerful script leads to a life of opportunity. As a child we have a blank script that is marked through our interactions as we grow. People might say you can't, you're not good enough, flip that script. You are what you think you are, not what they think you are! I was conditioned to play it safe. i felt i was always being compared to others, excluded because of my culture and heritage. The first step in flipping your script is to stop with the self-limiting narrative. How many times have you talked your way out of an opportunity? These limiting thoughts are damaging us from achieving our purpose and finding our music. The stories we tell ourselves form our identity and dictate what we believe we can and cannot do. Our inner world reflects our outer world. Reaching for perfection is like grabbing the wind. When we accept that we all make mistakes and failure is just a steppingstone to your next level. We don't allow failure to hold us back, use failure as a platform to fall forward. You face your own individual battles in life, you can hide from it or use it as a platform to grow from, to build resilience from. The person you see is the person you will be. In life we have more examples than I have space to write of people who overcame insurmountable odds to achieve their best in life. Once we let go of the past, let go of the self-limiting beliefs we can then grab a hold of our music and live our dream. You may have been conditioned to play it safe. Always been compared to others, brothers or sisters. I had to push through, by flipping the script.

In the early days of hip hop the pioneers wanted to stay fresh, to stay ahead of the game. If everyone could do it, then it wasn't fresh, if everyone was wearing it, then it wasn't fresh. It took research, I had to become a student of the game. I honed my skills and learnt new ways to present my skill set. How can I stay fresh so my music inside can be timeless? I soon realized that it was a must that I keep learning. As an artist it all began in my bedroom, it took practice and learning my craft so I could move from my bedroom to the largest arenas in the country. I studied successful emcees and replicated what they did. By doing me, I gave myself a platform for my inner voice to declare I am here, and this is my music. The more you learn the more you earn. I had to stay relevant and be in tune with the changes taking place in the scene and the ones that would take place in the future.

I knew if I didn't make noise who would make noise for me. We represented our brand and through word of mouth a silent voice became a scream. What started out local has gone global. Don't wait for permission, you make some noise. We had to make noise, say what needs to be said. Raise your voice above the negativity and limiting beliefs and shout we are here. We need to shout I can do this. I need to ask the question in the positive, 'why not me.' The foundations of hip-hop culture were birthed in low-income neighborhoods in the late 1970s where the artistic and cultural expressions of predominantly people of colour displayed a unique and imaginative response to oppressive and self-limiting conditions. In the same way you may face obstacles that have backed you into a corner. These setbacks may have brought you to your knees. Now is not the time to throw the towel in. Setbacks must be viewed as set ups for greater opportunities. In a matter of decades, the culture influenced, and has influenced every region on the planet. In the same way your music inside is equipped to influence way beyond your reach. In realizing that it might take a while for me to do what I truly love, I needed to make sure I was developing the right habits. This includes professional habits, like becoming a great networker and becoming a student so you are continually upgrading your skill set. I call it being on purpose, success is not an accident but a planned process. When practiced regularly over time, these habits will sustain you even when things get tough. As your journey progresses, you can always fall back on these learned and cultivated skills. We make noise by being on purpose.

To be on purpose is to be ready, doing the things successful people are doing. Setting goals should be like playing snooker. Each shot you make to be successful must set you up for the next shot. In a matter of decades, hip-hop culture has influenced, every region on the planet. In the same way your music inside, gives you the ability to influence way beyond your reach. It has become a formidable worldwide cultural phenomenon. In going worldwide, hip-hop has taken the anxiety, hope, social and political conditions of life in the inner cities to the international stage. It has become an anti-privilege culture, creating its own special style of communication, dress styles, and adopting a culture of resistance to institutional dominance, class exploitation, and middle-class values.

Hip hop gave me the platform to say, I AM HERE. It started as my unique way to express my love for life in all its intricacies. A way of releasing my music inside, connecting with my passion and joy.

Stories are an ancient form of human expression; they spark a connection that takes you on a journey. From the foundation of time, they have been used to preserve culture and values. A story is an event that is either fact or fiction that someone speaks. The listener experiences the journey and they can learn, be inspired and experience various emotions through this process. Stories can be like a mirror where we see our lives reflected in the words on the page or through the mouth of the orator. They ignite our imaginations and revive dreams long ago forgotten.

"Tell me the facts and I'll learn. Tell me the truth and I'll believe. But tell me a story and it will live in my heart forever."

Native American Proverb

It's the oldest story ever told. Underdogs achieving against the odds. People who have been forgotten and abandoned by everyone finding their music inside and inspiring the world. It is through finding their music inside that they found a voice and, in turn, allowed everyone in the world the ability to find their voice. We might have been underdogs, but once we discover who we are, there is a power that we can unleash. On stage, I connect with my true self. I'm a performer, I was made to inspire. Now I have to keep it real and be true to my music inside. As soon as you uncover the music inside the opposition, those age-old self-limiting beliefs attack your music from inside and out. It is a movement that has made those who were invisible visible. This is the impact that finding your music can have, not just on the individual but on the world. No matter where you are in life, when you find your music inside, you shout to the world, 'I AM HERE!' No longer someone that

29

struggles with who they are, but someone who lets the music inside play on full volume. How can you start your journey? In the same place I started mine, all great stories start with a first step. I got tired of trying to fit into someone else's puzzle space, I watched others release their music and I wanted to release mine.

I dared to dream in 84.

With a passion for hip hop I couldn't ignore.

I wanted it more than anything I had before.

LRS was born we dropped hard to the core.

Street wars to tours in 88.

In a climate of hate gave me a route to navigate.

On four track tapes the sound was iconic.

The styles the dress our words were symbolic.

The culture the scene the rage it was our tonic.

Bass lines so low the sound was subsonic.

The flows hypnotic, these jams were packed out.

> *Our stories getting told from the ends to packed*
> *crowds.*
> *I'm so proud, from true kings the truth brings.*
> *We move in, this new thing we doing, improving.*
> *We still grooving like you know what it means.*
> *Like you know what I've seen, like they know where I've*
> *been.*

I had a seed inside of me, but no one understood its potential. How far it could reach or what its impact could be. The purpose of a seed is to grow. Out of something so small and insignificant, I lived a transformation from disillusionment to hip hop pioneer. From a small insignificant seed to a tall elegant tree or beautiful flower. As soon as I began to dream, that little seed stirred inside me. The goals I set myself fuelled and watered my dream; the positive steps I was taking towards my dream brought it into the physical universe. That seed was the music inside me, it is this music that will define who I am and all I can be. When I lived my music, I was living on purpose, and my music was being played for all. My energy levels were maxing out. I toured for two years straight up and down the country with only one day off in the week. The feeling I used to have that something was missing went away when I found my music. The sense of fulfilment I experienced as I lived it was an amazing natural high. When you don't feel connected to your life, you lack purpose and the necessary passion to fulfil your dreams.

What was my purpose? Was it what the teachers said I would be? Was it the limits that society placed on me? I was made to live life to the fullest and that could only happen if I lived my music. I must be the me the world is waiting for. I searched for answers outside of myself to make sense of how I was feeling. I focused on occupations to find meaning. I was not going to give up even though I felt disillusioned at times. Something inside me was driving me forward.

I kept asking myself 'why am I here?' Was I living for what mattered to me, was I living my values? I wanted to inspire, I wanted to make a difference, I wanted to be centre stage, I just didn't know it yet. I wanted to know I was doing the right thing. It was so strange to grasp, rap was seen as a rebellious form of expression and yet it was my release into a passion-filled life

When we live as we were created to be, we show how unique and powerful we are. We ask the question, why am I here? Your answer lies within you. I'm here to breathe into the bigger story that is taking place. To blow over the internal flame in our souls so that passion and desire spring forth. This will lead to our greatest discovery, the reason for being. Our reason for being is greater than how we feel or have experienced so far. It's time to be part of a greater story. A story that will define who we are and give our lives purpose. I made the mistake when I thought it was all about my story, but I came to understand that a greater story has been unfolding since creation. I was not aware of the bigger story and how it intercepts our present reality, it dissects our stories at different times. I lived day by day not realising that every choice I made reached into eternity and had divine implications. We live once and how we live is determined by the choices we make. The first time I went on stage, I connected with my true self.

"There is no greater gift you can give or receive than to honour your calling. It's why you were born. And how you become most truly alive."

Oprah Winfrey

"You can only become truly accomplished at something you love. Don't make money your goal. Instead pursue the things you love doing and then do them so well that people can't take their eyes off of you."

Maya Angelou

We used to flow from the heart while uplifting the art.
Painting pictures with our words ripping hard beats apart.
Representing our ends, we grew from boys to men.
We knew the system was against us and it still is my friend.
Can't be killing my own, want to inspire my own.
On the streets there being hunted in the kill or be killed zone.
Articulate in a verse what it means to be young and black.
Inspire to fire on the road to the ends and back.
So listen the melody, the bass line it follows me.
You ask if I'm flowing well you know that I'm ready see.
YAHUAH's gift, it's turning the tide.
I'm ready to live, I've found the music inside.
I've found the music that drives,
The music inside makes my soul alive.

I was known as KG DEMO and I couldn't get enough of it, spending my Saturday mornings at Bluebird Records listening to the latest imports. I consumed hip hop whenever I could get it. Enjoying Mastermind Roadshow with Herbie cutting up the beats on the wheels of steel (Turntables). This inspired me to form our own sound system called 'Freakaristic.' We played at venues around the NW10 area of London. It was there we met Lepke and Daddy Ernie through the Dread Broadcasting corporation, we called it DBC. They got us a slot at Notting Hill Carnival. DBC was the first African–run pirate station in Britain. In those days most Jamaican reggae artist or producers who came to the UK made it a point to pass through Harlesden.

That was the first time I rhymed in front of a live crowd, August 28th, 1985. The sound evolved organically into a Rap group. By this time, I lived and breathed hip hop. Another sound system called 'Elite', whose DJ lived on the same road as Herbie from Mastermind, had slick skills. David Lovindeer (DJ DEE), Andrew Coulson (Playboy Prince) and me (KG Demo) had the idea of starting the London Rhyme Syndicate.

When I chose the name London Rhyme Syndicate, it was a controversial choice. In hindsight, I was naive with my choice as I didn't look to see if there were other crews with similar names and I didn't check Go-Daddy to see if the domain name was available. Today, you want your name to stand by its uniqueness. There was another crew from North London called the Sindecut, and they felt our names were too similar and we had stolen their name. We had already released 'Hard to the Core' and were booked for a show in Chalk Farm. It was a setup, they wanted to battle as they felt disrespected. The atmosphere was electric, we felt like something was going down. We were from Harlesden, so we didn't care; we were going on regardless. We were introduced and the crowd was silent apart from our people who came for us. The DJ made our record jump and the battle lines were drawn. They had the venue, the crowd and the final say. We dropped some rhymes in retaliation, and after that, we vowed never to be caught out like that again. We later found out that a young beatboxer who wanted to join our crew felt disgruntled and set the whole thing up. That was the beauty of hip hop, it gave us positive ways to settle our differences that were not violent. You would think creatively. This was done by writing raps that were directed as insults for the purpose of battling.

I wanted to be an artist who made music of the soul and was awakened to how powerful it could be. A poet relays emotion with words you can see and feel, a storyteller tells the story that is within them. An artist reveals what he sees inside himself, an advocate stands in defence of those in need of support. A teacher is the one who sees life as his classroom, they must all be what they have been made to be. We can get lost like a piece of a puzzle trying to force ourselves into someone else's picture. We can't see the bigger picture and lose our place within our personal story. This can have a dramatic effect on our well-being as we are made for a divine purpose. I pray you will shine your light, and as we gather our lights together, we will blaze. This blaze will see dreams awakened and potential realised as we live our life purposes in partnership with power. Then, as we find the music inside, we let it play without restraint!

"I am here again, in a familiar place feeling something I've felt before, wondering why it's still here, why I didn't deal with it more fully before. But I'm glad I have a second chance at it ... and I know that if I need a third chance, I'll get it. I also know that if it comes up again, I'll recognize it sooner and deal with it more readily. This is growth. And, I am happy to be alive."

Jan Denise

Everything was coming together; my creative, social and thought potential were meeting at this point. It was not about the money or becoming famous, although I would not have said no to any of those. It was about reaching my potential as a hip hop emcee, it was about achieving my dream.

There were times I couldn't sleep at night I was so excited about being what I dreamed. It felt like I was dreaming with my eyes open. On the stage I declare, **I AM HERE**. As soon as you uncover the music inside the opposition, those age-old self-limiting beliefs attack your music from inside and out and outside in. It transformed my status from the invisible to the visible. This is the impact that finding your music can have, not just on the individual but on the world. No matter where you are in life, when you find your music inside, you shout to the world, '**I AM HERE!**'

'If you don't know where you're going, any road will take you there.'

Reynolds

I wasn't made to fit in, I was made to stand out.

I AM HERE!

Chapter 2
Genesis

"So live as if you were living already for the second time and as if you had acted the first time as wrongly as you are about to act now!"

Viktor E. Frankl

Your reality doesn't define your dreams, your dreams define your reality. In the summer of 1989, I was standing on stage getting ready to be filmed for the hit pop show that was 'Top of the Pops'. Nicky Campbell introduced us, the London Rhyme Syndicate, and it was lights, camera, action. It felt like all eyes were on me as the music filled the air, creating the type of atmosphere that I thrived in. I was ready for this, it seemed my whole life, everything I had been through made sense at this defining moment. I looked good; the original UK Hip Hopper was in the house. Girls were screaming as I burst into rhyme, the words flowing like a wave and I was riding it like a seasoned artist. A crescendo of screams greeted me as I began to move to the beat. I was in the zone, it was like a snake charmer mesmerising the crowd, taking them to that place where dreams are formed. This wasn't your regular commercial pop icon; I was a rising voice in the UK hip hop scene. Fila tracksuit and Troop solution trainers were the order of the day, a flat top hairstyle was all the rage. From the heights of this commercial edifice, I allowed myself the freedom to dream, to visualise what could be. Simultaneously, as parts of my dream were being realised, others were beginning to fade. I thought I had arrived, this is it. Little did I know that this was the first death knell I would experience, good thing that I was resilient. Giving up was not an option, in fact, it never is where dreams are concerned. At this time, the commercial juggernaut had sharp teeth and no qualms in chewing you up and spitting you out. Success can be a fairweather friend that visits for a short time. As I look back, this was our most successful part of the journey. There is a saying that talent gets you there but its character that keeps you. Dealing with the bumps in the road help shape your character – as I would realise, it's not about doing but being. To tell you the truth, I enjoyed better performances in less prestigious venues. Why? They felt real and I was all about keeping it real.

I was a young creative rhymer with a love for hip hop. I belonged to a crew, and within that environment, my creative inclinations thrived. I wanted to express myself by producing rhymes and beats that moved the crowd, but I had limited resources. I never had the finances to have the equipment to make the journey as smooth as I desired. What I had was infused by an urban ground-breaking spirit, it was called hip hop. The culture of hip hop spread rapidly from the streets of New York to London and into the very consciousness of listeners and performers around the globe. Youth looking for an identity they could relate to were mesmerised by this new-found movement. Now, we describe it as a global movement crossing the hidden barriers and boundaries of culture, class and gender. It provided an awareness of cultural and social issues through positive and meaningful messages of inclusion, justice, and success. It empowered us in England to take a stand and it was a true pioneering spirit that rose to the challenges we were facing. We gave the places where we played positive role models and brought motivational messages that informed the listeners about relevant and positive life choices.

I was young and hard headed, ain't no black and I said it,

Drop the x pick up the cross was for the lost who don't get it,

See the word we've read it, the truth we wear like a garm,(garment)

Equipped with knowledge of the way the way that we

come armed,

Dropping bombs in songs for so long coming strong,

In the shadows of the mind where no thought belongs,

You see the path and react, my mind much deeper than

that,

I won't be bought by the lie that's designed to trap,

Like a foetus in labour, the waters ready to burst,

Ready for birth, visions of peace for residents of earth,

So we focus our dreams to keep in line with the times,

Words recorded in the booth revealing timeless lines,

Seeing youths with no prospects who will offer them

hope,

So many offer them dope there on a slippery slope,

So once again we come the revolution is on,

The revolution is on, this time we rise as one.

I am Basil Reynolds, formally known as KG DEMO. Today, they call me REYNOLDS. Raised by Jamaican parents who arrived into the UK during the

Windrush migration, settling in Harlesden in North West London. Their struggle and sense of pride will always be a source of strength that motivates me. It strengthens and defines me. My parents both had a faith and raised me with strong values and principles. My mum was a giver, she was a mother's mother. I think back fondly about the type of woman she was. Every Sunday, she made a roast dinner for us as a family and two elderly people on our road. She did that for over 10 years until they passed on. I saw the faith she talked about in action. I always remember carrying trays of food up my road as a kid. From my early childhood, she was a childminder as well as a short-term foster mother. She had so much to give, it was true faith in action. That type of giving imprints itself in you. My dad was in the Jamaican army as a young man. He served on a ship and the Jamaican regiment were given the menial tasks daily by the British Army. He faced institutional racism as the British Army officers treated him and the other

Jamaican soldiers as second-class citizens. It was during that time his inner activist was born. In his later years, he became an important member of the post office union. It was there he rallied for better pay and conditions for his fellow workers. I will always remember his work ethic, and at the weekends, he was at his allotment growing fresh vegetables for us as a family. He had a vision for us and laid the foundation for it to be achieved. My parents' unwavering faith always provided me with an anchor during my roughest times. They have been a great influence on my life, and I look forward to seeing them again.

I spent my days riding around Kensal Rise on my BMX. Thrill seeking at Meanwhile Gardens on all the jumps and watching the BMX racing at Latimer road. Roller skating was big in London, the guys buying the latest wheels so they could go faster. Once a week at Harrow leisure centre, we gathered together for the roller disco, everyone showing off their skills to the latest soul tunes. I left school without a clear direction for my life. I attended college for a year and a half but, unfortunately, my heart was not in it. I didn't want to become a Mechanical and Production Engineer. I only chose the course as it seemed like the logical step to take. My effort levels eroded as my heart was not engaged and my passion fire was smouldering. I tried various careers, engineering, graphic design, but nothing inspired me. I was going through the motions. Nineteen years old and no direction, I only came alive when I went out. I loved music, dancing, showing off my thing. Going to the Electric Ballroom and throwing down to the latest funk tunes. I didn't connect the two, career with what I loved. It felt like weekends were my escape. I was trapped in the week, and on the weekends, it was my release. Things soon changed for me. Hip hop as a movement has been described as the most important youth culture on the planet. A global language that translates to a global audience. It adapts to the arenas where culture and creative freedom thrives. I have been involved in the music game from the early eighties, experiencing the highs and lows of a business that has a reputation for not taking any prisoners. But it was hip hop that gave me the platform to find myself and express who I was to the world.

In the middle of my age I turn the page in a rage,

I engage every youth from every concrete cage,

It's the end of the days look at the ways then pray,

There's no delay and so I say let's change our selfish

ways,

Consuming more than we need, it's nothing but greed,

All the brands don't give a damn as they just

constantly feed,

Where getting fat from the load, watch the pride as it

grows,

Like Sodom we go, it will eventually blow,

See the divide as it grows, much quicker you know,

> *Governments they change and still the money don't*
>
> *flow,*
>
> *So we go live online with no signs you don't miss,*
>
> *When the pies divided up, we know my people get nish*
>
> *(nothing),*
>
> *It takes more than words to please us, he came to free*
>
> *us,*
>
> *Praise Yahusha he walks only fools don't believe us,*
>
> *So once again through the pain the revolution is on,*
>
> *The revolution is on, this time we rise as one.*

I spent my time listening to songs and writing rhymes. At that time, our recreational choices were limited, it was either the Commodore 64 or the Sinclair Spectrum. For me, it was a dose of hip hop in the morning, hip hop in the afternoon and hip hop through the night. I lived and breathed the scene, the music, the lifestyle, everything about it. If you want to see your dream fulfilled, you have to put the work in. Everywhere I went, I would be writing rhymes using all I saw and experienced as fuel for the fire that was burning within me. I watched as Hollywood got in on the act, hip hop hit the big screen with classics such as Beat Street, Krush Groove, Breakdance and Wild style. This only heightened my excitement for this expressive vocal and, as some reported, rebellious art form. The stereotypical caricatures never bothered me as they were already evident in society. I knew what I was and what I wanted my music to be and reflect, a young man from the streets of London.

> *You got to dance like they clock it, just simply rock it,*
> *Lighting fires on road, the code from Harlesden to*
> *Toxteth,*
> *See the struggle the same, still playing the game,*
> *The blood boils in my veins as we try to maintain,*
> *To get ahead wanting the chance to advance our lives,*
> *While many talk about their wealth I see so many die,*
> *They want to be like the best, they want a piece and be*
> *blessed,*

> *They lust the car that you drive and the way that you dress,*
>
> *No oasis in the ends, so they are dying of thirst,*
>
> *You take advantage of the need I hope the bubble it bursts,*
>
> *Never the norm in liquid form so now I'm burning it,*
>
> *So hot its scorching it, rising up as one is just a warning kid,*
>
> *It's like a horror show as you survey the scene,*
>
> *Mad dreams in the minds of power-hungry fiends,*
>
> *So once again we come the revolution is on,*
>
> *The revolution is on, this time we rise as one.*

Rap music started to outsell other genres of music and it was rapidly becoming the most influential art form, dictating and directing various trends. Major companies started to use the culture being created as a means of promotion for their products. It emerged in marketing campaigns, in advertising. Over the years, I have witnessed the movement's direct fashion trends, hairstyles, dialect, car choice, everyday mannerisms and I was a part of it. Like someone infected by a virus that was so contagious, it infected who I was and I had the privilege of passing it on. From musical preference to the way we greeted each other on the streets. From complex handshakes to shoulder-hugs, it was all theatre and we were the cast.

I went through many phases as hip hop evolved. During this process, I grew and matured as a rhymer. One thing never changed, which was my love for the art. I have always loved reggae music, it was the sound of my childhood. In the seventies, I remember West Indian families getting together, it was music, curry goat and jerk chicken. It was the culture I was birthed in. I listened to dancehall and the way the emcee's flowed during a soundclash. This was when two sound systems challenged each other to see who was the best. We took a mix of what the Ragga Emcees were doing and the rappers from the states and developed our own form of expression. It was our freestyle.

> We paint a picture of the city too, it's lacking truth,
>
> Promote the worst of the ghettos whose, blinding the youth,
>
> The ghetto life's a mirage, look at the way that they package it,
>
> The worst of the city so why are we proud of it,
>
> Thug life it is promoted because they hate you, it all degrades you,
>
> Who can save you if you're blind to what the hate do,
>
> So many make do with personas that are savage,
>
> Shredded like cabbage I said our minds are being ravaged,
>
> Treat ghettos like badges but ghettos are slums,
>
> Conditioned in the thought its where our heroes belong,
>
> Where our dreams get hung, but I tell you it's wrong,
>
> Picture a kingdom of kings that is where we are from,
>
> Not a nigga as it triggers racist thoughts from beyond,

> *Still I'm chosen by the one and still we hunted by guns,*
>
> *You see the time is gonna come when we'll all see the*
>
> *son,*
>
> *And realise that we've been lied to from the day we call*
>
> *one,*

The movement continued to evolve despite the efforts of the many haters who made it their mission to minimize the influence it was having on young people. Oppression builds resilience and strength and it only strengthened our resolve. The music was being listened to by young people throughout the world, regardless of their background or persuasion. When you viewed it through a mainstream media lens, it was a negative social art form. It's not just about gangster rap and woman-hating. For many, it's a way of life, a culture that is complexly woven into every aspect of their daily life. It helped shape the man I am today. The fact that my parents didn't understand it was a bonus as it enhanced the rebellion that I was going through; hip hop gave me an outlet to voice it safely. It was a new radical culture, one that accepted me for who I was. It brought new ideas, values and concepts that reflected how I wanted to live, in song, poetry, film, dance, a piece of art or fashion. It was us on the street corner just hanging out, freestyling as someone made a beat. Some would pull out a piece of lino they had brought and spontaneously burst into dance. Others were climbing onto the train tracks in the cloak of darkness and produced masterpieces on the sides of trains and bridges.

The world is changing at a speed we cannot truly comprehend. Social media has changed the way we communicate and has developed a language of its very own; it has changed the boundaries and levelled the playing field. Now young people are making tracks and shooting videos and uploading them onto social media sites. They can cause a worldwide buzz from their bedrooms. iTunes and YouTube have given each artist a means to get their product out and begin to make an impact upon the mass market. Social media has seen the rise of young entrepreneurs who have mastered the technology and have learnt how to build a foundation from which they can establish a future. We have also seen the rise of reality shows like Big brother and the Voice. Now we see reality music shows that showcase tomorrow's stars today. They market an artist and see which one the public support and the winner will already have a huge fan base who will buy their first single. It's a win-win situation for those behind the scenes.

It seems that the music industry has always been more about who you know than the talent you possess. We used to joke that labels hated real artists as they were harder to mould and shape; if it was puppets they wanted, it was puppets they would get. They preferred the individual who would sing what they wanted, dress how they wanted and be what they wanted them to be. To follow the trends that were established, not pioneer new pathways. The money men want the least risk on their return. That is what I told myself, it could be my truth or the truth, it didn't matter. I had a vision and mission to fulfil.

I had no excuse for what I did, I didn't need one. It was brilliance birthed by a rawness that gave each track its own cutting edge. This was done by us first assessing the situation then simplifying it. It made sense to those who had no experience of the inner-city streets or life we lived. From random groups, the idea became a vision and the vision was born into a movement that has gathered momentum. We made mistakes along the way, but I achieved so much in the processes of expression.

To succeed, you need to find something to hold on to, something to motivate you, something to inspire you.
Tony Dorsett

You must be the change you want to inspire. My reputation, my character, and my behaviour needed work. First, I needed it to happen inside me. The only

60

way to call the best out of others is to expect the best from yourself. I needed the invitation into the bigger story that has always been unfolding. Stories don't tell people what to do, they give you something to follow. They engage people's imaginations and emotions. They show people what they're capable of becoming. I was beginning to see that I could be more than I had been. I was inspired by hip hop, how a group that lacked identity found it through a creative art form. How it transformed popular culture. I wanted more, I wanted to see a transformation inside me. It was my journey; my footprints and it was my music inside. I knew I needed to breakout. Society's expectations for me would not come close to those I have of myself. I am a dreamer! What I do may not be what you were expecting; it may be something beyond your wildest expectations. Antoine de Saint-Exupéry, the French aviator and author of "The Little Prince", wrote,

"If you want to build a ship, don't drum up the men to gather wood, divide the work and give orders. Instead, teach them to yearn for the vast and endless sea."

I was a dreamer, I dreamed of being a rap icon. I longed to be on stage, I wanted it so bad I could taste it. An atmosphere was created inside of me that caused me to conceive and give birth to my dream. Since its inception, hip hop has surpassed its role as a voice and has become something more, just as I have believed I could be more. Philosopher, Frantz Fanon, once wrote: *"Each generation out of relative obscurity must discover their mission, fulfil it or betray it"*. Go hard in the direction of your dreams and I hope you enjoy the journey.

Chapter 3
Memory Lane

Life can only be understood backwards; but it must be
lived forwards.
Life is not a problem to be solved, but a reality to be
experienced.
Søren Kierkegaard

The eighties was the era defined by greed; a time of prosperity and rising house prices. The word Yuppie entered our language, meaning a young, upwardly mobile professional. T.V Evangelists started speaking more about wealth and termed it the prosperity gospel. The prosperity was not equally shared as I saw for myself in what is called the North-South divide. I realised that capitalism is the hidden plutocracy. As I travelled the country performing, it became more apparent. Black people lived in the ghettos in Leeds, Cardiff, Manchester,

Liverpool, Bristol and Birmingham. Whenever I performed, I wanted to give them something that would inspire them, a light relief from the struggle.

Britain's first female Prime Minister was in power, strikes were happening around the country, but my focus was on the next song. It was during this time the country suffered a severe recession. To tell you the truth, it made no difference to me as I was already in recession. The struggle would continue. Many businesses failed and unemployment was reaching record levels. The Iron lady's severe policies and forceful use of the police caused civil unrest. Violent disturbances broke out in Toxteth in Liverpool, Brixton in London, and Moss Side in Manchester. It seemed that the country was falling apart but, in truth, the oppressed were saying that they had enough. Just seeing her image on TV filled me with resentment. As the era ended, the new-found prosperity was unravelling. For me, nothing changed,

I just went on living the best I could with limited resources.

Fresh out of the riots in 1981, we were headed into fresh controversy. On 28 September 1985, in South London, it was going to be the area's second riot in four years. I was nineteen years old and angry. It was sparked by a police officer shooting Cherry Groce. She was in bed when the police came calling, looking for her son. She was shot as they raided her home. This was the tipping point for the community. Protests quickly turned to hostility between the large crowd and the police. The battle was carried out on the streets of Brixton. It was like a war zone as young people held running battles with the police. Masked youths throwing petrol bombs were the iconic image of that time. Little to no airtime was given to the Groce family. The police officer who shot her was prosecuted, but as was and is the norm, he was acquitted of malicious wounding. One week later, another serious conflict sparked by similar circumstances in Tottenham was the fire that sparked the Broadwater Farm riot. Cynthia Jarret was pushed over during an illegal search on her home. She suffered a heart attack in the process. Once again, the community said enough is enough. During the riots, PC Keith Blakelock was murdered by an unidentified group. In their pursuit to find the killer, the police forged statements and used illegal interrogation techniques to get a confession. Three young men were charged with the murder and later acquitted. The atmosphere in the country felt tense and was imbedded into a conscious psyche.

Technology jumped forward as computers became accessible to the working class. The world saw the mobile phone for the first time and it quickly became the symbol of the time. These non-essential items made me forget the fact that life was not what it should be. From being token items, they quickly became essentials for us all and we have been convinced we can't live without them. The music of the time was Punk, for Britain's rebellious teens. Some identified themselves as Mods and made their weekend pilgrimages to Carnaby Street. It was during this backdrop that hip hop was transmitted to the UK and broke the recognised cultural boundaries. The old boundaries were about to be replaced with a more inclusive arena that would give us a cross-cultural arena. But let's go back to the early days of the scene. I was captivated by the animated colours and booming base sounds of hip hop. Colourful hats with large hi-top trainers with different coloured laces. The hip hop pioneers were characters that were larger than life. Not only sound but it was a fashion revolution in an era where social revolution was commonplace. What started in the ghettos of Harlem crash-landed in the UK at the Lyceum theatre with Dougie Fresh and Slick Rick and Grandmaster Flash. It was like a fever spreading through the inner city; it was a case of who wouldn't be infected by this. I was sixteen years old in 1983 and the hot tune was 'The

Perfect Beat' by Africa Bambaata and the Soulsonic Force. Where you find the oppressed, you will always find a creative means of expression. Some communicated with an aerosol can, those who appreciated the scene through visual masterpieces. Others displayed a flash of footwork wizardry with a touch of rhythm that also produced bodily moves that embraced the beat. For those like me, I used forceful wordplay. The DJ used programmed beats for orchestrating the crowd, and when it was all put together, it created one voice, it was hip hop. The early shows were collective events with singers, dancers, DJs, and graffiti artists. It was how we communicated truth. This was in opposition to mainstream news outlets who had failed us; this new movement was rapidly becoming a voice!

The first time I dipped my feet into the world of hip hop was at a warehouse in West Hampstead. It was the Mastermind Roadshow; these guys were the real deal. Herbie was scratching and transforming live during his set. The crowd was going crazy for it; I was going crazy for it. Smoke machines added to the atmosphere. The evening ended with a performance by Sidewalk. They were the premier body popping and breakdance crew in the UK. They never disappointed, spinning on their backs, hands and heads. Manipulating their bodies to create new moves, it was all British and very inspirational.

It gave me a route to escape the low aspirations I was so often saddled with. The limiting beliefs society thought they would assign to me. Hip hop was a mesh of styles and music genres that formed this new sound and look. We took something that existed in one form and made it our own. We broke all the rules they imprisoned us behind to launch our hearts on an unsuspecting audience. I wanted people to see through their ears every time I constructed a verse. We never played by the rules that mainstream music stood by. DJs not only extended tracks, they used the cross-fader to manipulate and create sounds to create unique rhythms. Emcees complimented those rhythms with melodic poems detailing the life and trials of growing up in their respective neighbourhoods.

Graffiti artists took spray cans and painted masterpieces using walls and bridges as a canvas. B-Boys danced, performing acrobatic moves that defied gravity. I witnessed the creative ability of self-taught young people, many who were failing within their local educational system. They took something that was available, accessible and affordable and created something positive as an alternative to the negativity they were burdened with. It addressed what mainstream education in the UK has never dared to address: the identity of a black youth – my identity. It created a style of its own, a look, a way of communicating, a swagger that could be seen in Sierra Leone and in Brixton at the same time. It directed youth culture, and that has been the case in my life. The influence we had over the wider youth culture is without precedent. Born out of the struggle; you can tell where a society is at by the music they produce and consume. Hip hop is no different. I was a product of the eighty's scene, part of that first generation of emcees in the UK. We were influenced by the sound that came out of Harlem and Kingston. It was edgy and best fitted my current plight. The fact that my parents were Jamaican meant I was immersed in the sounds of the West Indies. The sound systems like Saxon, Java Hi Power, and Sir Coxsone inspired me, but it was the sound of Harlem that provided the platform for me to enter the stage. I first performed at Notting Hill carnival in 1984 and it was the first time I pushed myself forward to enter the struggle of the rhymer. It was hot, and I don't mind saying, so was I. That's when I realised I found the music inside, my calling to articulate my story over hard-core beats.

My mind often drifts back, I need to remind myself at times that realizing our dreams are possible. I see young people and the impact of crushed hopes and dreams. I wonder what their music would sound like, what our communities are missing out on. At times I sit down with my head in my hands. You know the feeling when things build up. I want to explode like a bottle of Champagne that has been violently shaken. I have to take a deep breath, manage my emotions. I have known too many young people that have never seen there eighteenth birthday. I see young men and young woman, I want to shout, to get their attention. I want to let them know all they need to succeed in life is inside them. Sometimes the powers that be only see what they want to. We have so many role models in the most unusual places. Many of their stories are only being spoken by word of mouth. We must remember our stories and pass them on.

It all begun for me in 84

LRS crew, we dropped 'Hard to the core'

The time was iconic the whole planet was on it

Like any other rapper the stage was our tonic

Our profile organic, open mics the hype,

The breakers illuminated some ridiculous styles

Abandoned spaces the places where we got down

Rapperattack, Freshbeat and Mastermind with the

sound

The atmosphere was toxic we lick shots in the air

DJs on the 2 techniques were getting ready to tear

With flare I swear, we dropped facts in stacks

Dave pierce, Westwood, Pogo, Swift and Nat

Mc battles as the rappers went crew for crew,

Mainstream ignored us as the culture grew

The rhyming, breaking, the DJs playing,

Art on walls, kicking knowledge no delaying

The first rap I recorded was called 'Hard to the Core.' When I heard it for the first time on the radio it was exhilarating, I can say it was one of the best feelings I have experienced. I listened to it nonstop for days and nights. I was too excited to sleep; my creation was being played. I wanted everyone to hear it so they could feel the way it made me feel. The feedback in the music papers was positive and encouraging. I found my music and what I wanted to do with my life.

Rhyming didn't depend on my economic state, I would sit around showcasing my latest rhymes to anyone who would listen. I listened to every hip hop record I could get my hands on. I would sit about chilling, dreaming, visualising the success and suddenly be brought crashing down to earth by my current situation. I had to learn to see with my imagination. Slowly but surely, everything I did revolved around music.

Dancers battle against other dance crews, and DJs would cut and scratch to see who the fastest and cleanest mixer out there was. Even graffiti artists would put their pieces up against other graffiti crews. I would go around the clubs battling emcees to see who the best was. It was a test of your rhyme vernacular, one against one, like two boxers going at it in the ring. To build a reputation as a rapper, you would have to enter battles and rap competitions that the radio DJs would put on and hope to come out victorious. Tim Westwood would run a weekly competition on Capital Radio; you had time constraints to put a verse together on a chosen subject. The winner would be invited to their studios to record a live session. It was the biggest hip hop show in the country. One of our crew named Little Prince Jay phoned in and won it. The next week, we were dropping bars on the Westwood show. When I arrived at Capital Radio, I was taken into a small booth where we set up our turntables. We dropped

75

what soon became our signature song, 'Hard to the Core'. This immediately elevated our status as emcees.

The following year at Notting Hill carnival, I came back with a crew and I came back so much harder. Meanwhile, Gardens was packed as the crowd chilled in the sunshine. This time when I took to the stage, I treated it like I owned it. The crowd swayed in the afternoon sun and I directed their movement like a conductor of a grand orchestra. That performance caught the attention of Longsy Dee. He was a hip hop reggae artist who had a small studio and wanted to record us, it was an opportunity we could not turn down. I had nothing to lose and everything to gain. It gave me the opportunity to record 'Hard to the Core'. It quickly became popular on the underground scene. As soon as the track started, the crowd would go wild. Everyone knew it was L.R.S. We were introduced to Edward Christie who ran Abstract Records in Kensal Rise and had the

Cool Notes on his roster. He listened to our demo and put us into the studio. We recorded 'Hard to the Core' and Edward decided to give us our own label. Rhyme and Reason was born. I said every rhyme should have a reason. We followed Hard to the Core with our E.P, London Rhyme Syndicate. At this time, we toured the UK continually building an underground fan base. We were introduced to Trenton Harrison who was managing the Wee Papa Girl Rappers who headed up Rush Europe. I'm getting ahead of myself. From rapping over someone's beat, Hard to the Core had evolved into our calling card, it was our sound.

> *We went on strong we couldn't stop*
> *Hitting all your turf with a verse until it pops*
> *Double goose down, kango and troop solution*
> *Fila trackie on my back a natural revolution*
> *Evolution of rhyme in a line in my head,*
> *Every beat of my heart says it won't be dead*
> *The birth of the crews and they ain't done*

> *Hijack, Demon Boyz, Overlord and Phase One*
>
> *She Rockers, Wee Papa, Monie Love and Betty Boo*
>
> *MC Duke, MC Mello and the Cookie crew*
>
> *London Posse, Blade, the Sindecut and Derek B,*
>
> *The Brother movement inspired me,*
>
> *Simon Harris the Music of Life stable,*
>
> *independent vs major labels, major fables,*
>
> *Creative minds are able, turn the tables,*
>
> *Your views of the times enabled, rock the cradle,*

Pirate radio stations played the track building the buzz in the underground scene. It was a real trip to be in a club and witness the reaction to my music. Seeing the ravers with smiles on their faces as they got down was rewarding for all the hard work. You would even see the ones who had seen our performances and were copying our dance moves. It inspired me to work harder and dream bigger. I practised as hard as I could; I wanted to be at my best every time I performed.

The next phase was promotion. We phoned all the DJs, trying to persuade them to plug the song. We hit clubs like Club Savannah in Brighton, Tiffany's in Great Yarmouth, Martha's Vineyard in Swansea and many more around the country. I remember our performance at Martha's Vineyard. On our arrival, we received a police escort into the venue. The club promoters had to place a ring of bouncers around the stage as they feared we would be mobbed. I remember the crowd pushing onto the ring of security guards around the stage. The girls screamed all the way through our set. Every time I got near the edge of the stage, girls were trying to pull me off the stage, reaching beyond the cordon to grab me. That show was bouncing from start to finish. It reminded me of another venue, The Robin Hood Public House in Dagenham. Hordes of young girls rushed me after the show as I made my way back to the changing rooms. They managed to get my tracksuit top and trainers. The security had to search people on the way out to get my things back. This type of love can be intoxicating, and it is during these times I had to learn about staying balanced and not get gassed up on the vibes.

As a group, we went through a phase of building as we continued purchasing equipment until we had what we needed to produce good quality live shows and demos. The iconic 808 drum machine and the Akai S900, 2 Technics turntables and the phonic mixer were the essential tools to develop our own sound. I spent every penny I had on breakbeat albums as I fine-tuned my art in the bedroom. Every dream exacts a price from you. If you're not willing to sacrifice for your dream, it will not be realised.

I remember it was 89

LRS crew and D-Mob combine

It's time to get funky top of the pops

Game changers in danger cause the beat don't stop

Now where hall of famers from the underground

If you're down you're in the realm of the maniacal

sound

We had cause, no pause on tour we got hyper,

Mc's on the mic like lyrical snipers

Chrome Angelz, spraying the art, displaying their craft,

Styles on the side of a train as it pass,

B-Boy crews represent like the London All Stars

Sidewalk, their skills were hard

Chad Jackson, Herbie, Cutmaster Swift,

Rock the fader back and forth all crew don't riff,

Scared stiff of the science we kicked, battles we ripped,

The elements legit I remember the hits.

The Brother movement I give respect.

True music I will always select.

We rocked crowds from Scotland to Southend.

> *A young crew from west London representing to the end.*
>
> *Normski taking pictures as the beat goes on.*
>
> *My connection with Hip Hop will always be strong.*
>
> *Rush Europe I remember the days.*
>
> *Ah Yeah was how I entered the stage".*

I was given a flier about a rap competition at the Oasis night club in Dalston, London. The prize was a live session on Tim Westwood's show. We were pumped and dreamed of what the airplay could do for us. His was a prime-time national show and its reach was beyond what we could have hoped for at the time. We focused all our efforts on polishing our performance. The competition was going to be broadcast live on the radio. We went through various ways of performing it as we knew it would be key to get the crowd involved. When we entered the venue, we were glad we had practised because the stage was so small, we couldn't get our dancers on it. We positioned them at the front of the stage facing the crowd, they were in the crowd. As we were introduced, we made a thing of being as close to the crowd as we could. We wanted them to be a part of it. Our backing track started, and as we walked around the stage, we high-fived all the people in the front. The crowd went mad as we threw down 'Hard to the Core', it was a memorable night. We even stopped it early as I shouted 'rewind' to start it again. The crowd love a little showmanship. The venue was packed and the atmosphere was positive. We used a part of Gwen McCrae's 'All This Love That I'm Giving' for the chorus, it was a classic rare groove song and the crowd loved it. I put everything into it, I had no voice after it. The crowd had the power to influence the judges and they made so much noise for us. We won it, the judges on the night were Danny D and Tim Westwood. It would be Danny D who we would collaborate with later on with 'It is Time to Get Funky'. It was an epic night and we developed a close working relationship with CJ Carlos, the resident DJ in Oasis on a Sunday night. He also played on Time Radio and brought us in on his show. We continued to build a name. Through DJs like Chris Nat, Chris Forbes, Jasper the Vinyl Junkie; they pushed our tracks. We answered calls live on the radio to build our reputation. The only place success comes before work is in the dictionary.

We hit clubs like Club Savannah in Brighton and Tiffany's in Great Yarmouth. Another memorable show for me was Basildon Festival Hall. We were supported by the Jungle Brothers and Queen Latifah, we had a good following in Essex. We hit what I called the gravy circuit as it was the meat and gravy for a hard-working performer like me. Some of the venues I performed in were so run down, it was a miracle they were given licenses. It was work before success; I endured long nights and no sleep as it slowly became evident what was required to succeed. Touring brought us closer together and helped me form a positive work ethic. I can truly tell my children to chase their dreams and I remind them it won't be easy.

Chapter 4
A Search for Meaning

"No man can rise to fame and fortune without carrying others along with him. It simply cannot be done."

Napoleon Hill

Michael J Fox said; *'No matter how much fame you have, it's not something that belongs to you. If I'm famous, that doesn't belong to me -- that belongs to you. If you can't remember who I am, I'm no longer famous.'*

I opened my eyes, it was still dark and backstage was softly lit. My senses heightened; I was so pumped, everything else seemed like it was in slow motion. Something instinctively told me that I had to seize the moment, it was now or never. My heart felt like it was going to explode; it felt like everyone could hear it. Breathing in the cocktail of alcohol, perfumes and tobacco only strengthened my resolve. The building was animated, the ceiling sweating from the toxic atmosphere within. I looked at my Gucci timepiece and quickly straightened my clothes. It was organised chaos and I was its architect. They call me KG Demo and I write rhymes. The whole venue was alive, swaying back and forth like a snake. The bass line was hypnotic, sending its hungry listeners into a trance. The music was building to a crescendo. This was my hour. The arena erupted into a near-deafening eruption of pure emotion. The curtain rolled back as I made my entrance.

I had no choice but to give up the 9 to 5 and follow the music in my heart. I sensed that I was destined for more than I had so far achieved. I am here for a reason, now I need to walk in it. I cannot live to work, I work to live. What would my family say about me pursuing a fledgling career in rap? It wasn't even an accepted art form. How would I make money? *To fulfil any dream, you must first wake up.* There were no career paths that I desired to follow; all I had was the desire to be more than what they told me I could be. *Amateurs built the Ark and professionals built the Titanic,* so expect the unexpected. We can't be afraid to express who we are.

My first professional appearance on stage taught me a harsh lesson. We were supporting Cash Money and Marvellous at the Astoria Theatre in Tottenham Court Road, London. It was packed with people from all over; there wasn't even room to lift your arms. What an opportunity to announce ourselves as this new rap crew from London – instant stardom awaited us. I nervously watched the crowd. Tim Westwood introduced us and the crowd roared as we strolled onto the stage. Before I could speak, the backing track jumped, and then it jumped again. To make things worse, the crowd eventually turned. They booed us like we were pantomime villains on the stage. From a state of ecstasy to despair all in a matter of seconds. I walked off stage with my whole world in pieces, I felt like a failure. Wisdom takes every experience and uses it as building blocks to pave the way for a better tomorrow. Every professional was first an amateur.

Success is to be measured not so much by the position that one has reached in life as by the obstacles which he has overcome while trying to succeed.'
Booker T. Washington.

Your character will make you or break you. I remember an incident that took place at the Powerhouse in Birmingham. I loved touring, doing what I loved every day. We developed a tribe from all over the country. I treated the stage as my own, regardless of time or place, under strobe lights and pulsing speakers, thousands of screaming fans would greet me. They clapped with me, jumped with him, and when we did our call and response, they roared with me. The dressing room description would be, clean but cramped. It had a table with sandwiches and drinks. We left the Champaign unopened until the after show. I sat on the sofa to chill before I got changed. The venue provided a small stereo, we played the music we wanted to get us in the vibe. After an hour and a half on the motorway, we wanted to chill out. We had been on Top of the Pops, we were getting used to girls hanging about backstage. We had a knock on our changing room door. The club security brought in two girls in long fur coats followed by a man. They walked in, tall and blonde, they looked like models. Friendly smiled as the club manager introduced them to us. Autographs and signed pictures as well as some pictures with us. I thought nothing of it, we were used to requests like these. My mind distracted by the night's performance. We had done this frequently before, i was getting edgy before the show. I always had the nerves in my stomach. my eyes came out of their sockets as they removed their coats, revealing a tight bikini lingerie style. Surprised would be an understatement. Prinz cracked a joke and the look they gave him showed they were no fans of ours. The hair on my neck began to tingle; they seemed to be looking down on us. My mind went into overdrive. I shook my head; I asked them what you doing here, and they just kept smiling and motioning to the guy with the camera. Prinz blocked the cameraman from taking pictures. I told them to leave; I wanted to focus on the show. Later that night, one bouncer revealed that they always did this, and we saved ourselves being touted as the latest rappers with bad behavior. Frequently these girls caught performers in compromised situations and had the pictures to prove it. The wrong choice that day would have resulted in a front-page scandal. Hold on to your values as they will keep you in the game for the long haul. Some people will do anything for 5 minutes of fame or money. I don't know what their agenda was, but I would not be compromised by gold diggers.

It takes a lifetime to build a reputation and only one action to destroy it. How we respond to situations outside of us is key to staying in your music. I know my inner world shapes my outer, but at times, I let my outer shape my inner world. We were booked to do a show in Torquay. It would be our first time performing on the south coast. We hired three cars for the journey and I remember it took hours to get there. Our sound check was for 7.30 pm and we made it for 7.25 pm. We approached the stage entrance and were greeted by two bouncers blocking our entry. They said the club had a no trainer policy. We explained we were performing but they refused to budge from their position. Our tour manager asked to speak to the promoter. He was apologetic and said it was the club protocol. I laughed, they booked the London Rhyme Syndicate and failed to check out our style of dress. The bouncers were laughing at us, my outer was in control. I went from zero to one hundred in seconds. I allowed myself to get drawn in as I felt the need to defend myself. My brother intervened, explaining to the bouncers we were still going to be paid in full and they would also have to provide compensation for our meals. I was too angry to focus clearly, not enough oxygen to my brain. I couldn't let it go. I was angry in the restaurant and all the way home. The truth is, those bouncers had a laugh and then they forgot about us. I allowed their world view, their rottenness, to penetrate me and consume my emotions. I didn't want to jeopardise my future on the basis of someone else's limited belief. I only have room for mine and I came to the realisation that it was my choice. I wanted to be on stage to entertain, and at some point during the show, make a difference. I understood that I needed to develop self-actualisation. I had to be what I was made to be, and for that to take place, I have to learn and grow. I didn't want to conform to society's norms, I want to play my music. I wanted my light to shine. I learnt through this that I had to stay in my centre as other people's centres could be like injecting a virus into my system.

I felt like an underdog but the feeling of being on stage was my driving force for change.

We celebrate resilience and are encouraged when individuals overcome against the odds. We cheer on the underdog even though we haven't followed the progress. What do these concepts stir up inside us? What does it say about how we feel about ourselves? For some, the concept of the underdog is passed on from our environment. Our aspirations are set by them and the educational structure that builds us. We are never taught about money, its value, how it is used and invested. We are taught to be a part of the workforce. Within this narrow lane, our creativity is neutralised. We equate intelligence to what is a function of our memory and take on what they say we are. This keeps many trapped without the skills to navigate a way beyond the poverty trap. Poverty can be a mind-set established by generations of struggle. When you lack the ability to problem solve and think critically, you lack the skills to escape the poverty trap. An entrepreneur thinks outside the box, we must develop an entrepreneurial mind in all we do.

It is better to create something that others criticize,
Than to create nothing and criticize others.
Ricky Gervais

My art was not about how many people like my work. Your art is about the heart. It's about how honest you are with yourself. Never trade your identity for someone else's idea of success. You set the parameters of success and those measurements always lie within you. Your art lies within you, that creative spark that energises you is within you. When you tap into that energy, you are not framed by disappointment or how many people liked your work. You are framed by your heart. You understand the world needs your uniqueness; it needs you!

As a creative, I take you on a journey, I want you to identify on an emotional level with my heart. Heart recognises heart and has a unique way of making your creation timeless. It transcends boundaries and cultures as hearts connect hearts. Art is in the heart and from the heart and for the heart.

> *The road is narrow that I travel on and so I carry on,*
>
> *I got to find the place where I belong, before I'm gone,*
>
> *No other transport, but the walk I'm on, I'm being strong,*
>
> *Unfinished business in this world you know that's what I'm on,*
>
> *Came back a veteran, a better one who's better than,*
>
> *What I was before I'm repping like, was never done,*
>
> *To be the one, son of a gun you know I told you this,*
>
> *Not just an ego wanting more that's why I raise my fist,*
>
> *Look at the world I'm in, no fear I just want out of it,*
>
> *Before I go leaving my prints so you can follow it,*
>
> *Too much pain how can I gain within the lane I'm in,*
>
> *The flesh is weak to overcome so I'm battling,*
>
> *The process of releasing providing relief in,*
>
> *The day to day struggles believing I'm achieving,*
>
> *It is hardest for an artist in the darkness*

> *This music is a means of catharsis.*

Am I a product of my parents? They were resilient. They overcame the harsh emotional terrain in the late fifties in England. It would be easier to give up, but they stood their ground and rose above it. That is the type of character you draw upon after any type of setback. What I thought was a setback and what I thought was rejection was not. I was being redirected to something better.

I dreamt of being a voice, but what does that mean? I grew up without a dialogue, we lived in the shadows. Our experience was only shared in secret as we were bombarded with neutralising stereotypes. Certain newspapers like the Sun led the way with its racist narrative, diluting the black experience to demeaning caricatures. We needed voices to speak out and represent the unrepresented, even if what is being said is confrontational. I dreamed about being a voice. What I needed could not be attained in a seat of higher learning; it would only be diluted or misdirected. Before anything has been achieved, it carries with it the title of 'never been done'. The word possible is in impossible! This was all about being true to self – I was in the process of self-actualising. I thought about my mum. She was always the voice of reason when no one else understood or even wanted to. This was for her, for the support during the times when no one else could see what I could. She always said, "If you don't know where you're going, any road will take you there". She inspired me to dream and then encouraged me to chase it. The support she gave me allowed my confidence to push my desire.

'The man who makes a success of an important venture never wails for the crowd. He strikes out for himself. It takes nerve, it takes a great lot of grit; but the man that succeeds has both. Anyone can fail. The public admires the man who has enough confidence in himself to take a chance. These chances are the main things after all. The

man who tries to succeed must expect to be criticized. Nothing important was ever done but the greater number consulted previously doubted the possibility. Success is the accomplishment of that which most people think can't be done.'

C. V. White

Life is an unpredictable series of beginnings and endings. I know so many whose endings happened before they could leave their mark on this world. Raised in the nurturing grounds of North West London in a multi-cultural community, school life was quick and painless, and I seemed to avoid most of the stereotypes we were labelled with at the time. Young black men were routinely stopped and searched by the police. It always amazed me that such a small proportion of the population made up such a high proportion of those failing.

But today, it was my time and the crowd were looking to me for inspiration. A new artist was beginning his journey. The crowd were all throwing their hands in the air. It was organised mayhem, like the ecstasy witnessed on a Saturday afternoon at so many football stadiums around the country. It was their way of approving the lines I was rhyming. At that moment, we were all one. I lock eyes with those in the front row, I get the impression they get this as much as I do. My grip tightens around the microphone as I pace around the stage like a hungry predator. I didn't care about the critics; most of them have never played the game. Mere spectators who never risk anything apart from the time they take to strip the bravery of another.

While growing up, I saw so many people working hard with little reward. They have mortgages which translate into a debt they can barely afford. I don't see many enjoying their time or enjoying their families. Work gets the best of them, it slowly defines them, and people buy into it. They become lawyers, doctors, teachers and the list goes on. The reality is that we are first fathers and mothers, brothers and sisters, sons and daughters. It is our family and the choices we make that define us. Finding our music is finding our purpose. It is coming to that place where we realise we are more than what we do. I always remember seeing the local drug dealer cruising in his seven series BMW back in the day, rolling with a swagger like he was untouchable. His image became what all the kids wanted to be, the ghetto role model. Kids aspired to reach this by selling weed, robbing, whatever it took. Many without positive role models to look too as they searched for approval. Looking for someone to authenticate their manhood. I found mine through the pioneers of hip hop. They had status and wealth achieved not through hustling drugs but by rhyming a verse. Urban street poets revealing life stories that had long been buried. For some, these stories were uncomfortable listening as it reveals the true state of society. I had a simple dream, to care for my family and friends. For some, there is nothing more alluring than the forbidden. Some have painted a picture that less fortunate young people have idolised and immortalised over time, which has led to a misrepresentation of the music and the message that is within the music. We all live with the temptation of new things being flaunted and thrown in our faces. The latest phone, nicest car, games console, trainers, jacket and we are made to feel incomplete without it.

If you take it too deep the shallow peeps are confused,

Talk money and the power you get millions of views,

So much tension that I mention that we're pawns in the game,

Frauds will never explain, they know the game is insane,

To misdirect us, they supply us with the drugs to escape,

Alcohol is on the rise as our souls are raped,

> *Money and fame the new high that we inject from the*
>
> *source,*
>
> *Fake beauty in the eye of the surgeon of course,*
>
> *A fickle life fam, it's not intended to be,*
>
> *Take it back to the essence only then are we free,*
>
> *So believe me when I say this and I'm telling you*
>
> *straight,*
>
> *No matter what you desire stay away from hate,*
>
> *It's too late, sold a dream we could never attain,*
>
> *Or maintain the desire as it rots the brain,*
>
> *I explain it is hardest for an artist in the darkness*
>
> *This music is a means of catharsis.*

I could see the finishing line. I walked off the stage with the crowd screaming for more. I couldn't speak any more, I just wanted to drink down every ounce of this. I had the gift of the gab, it got me into trouble when I was young, and finally, I had found my purpose.

> *This music is a means of catharsis,*

> *Lighting up the way in the darkness,*
>
> *This music is a means of catharsis,*
>
> *Where making a way for the heartless.*

I sat there with a towel around my head thanking those who went before me, who inspired me. Rappers like Melle Mel, Kurtis blow, Grandmaster Kaz, the World Class Wrecking Crew, Public Enemy, Run DMC, Eric B and Rakim and LL Cool J. Now, I was amongst the elite. In the UK, it was Derek B, Phase ONE, Hijack, London Posse, Nutriment, Overlord X, MC Duke, the Demon Boyz, the Cookie Crew, the Sindecut – the birth of the UK scene was in full effect. Mainstream clubs shut their doors on us but now they were booking us for shows. Now they paid us to go to their clubs. That night defined me, I was twenty years old and ready to walk with giants.

Define the chosen who get frozen in the motions of life,

We got the notions that the potions used are nothing but lies,

I realise we in our prime the time that's passing us by,

I know the curse that's on my people worse as so many die,

It was YAHUAH who had chosen, origins of our line,

It is the devil who has woven in a coven of lies,

There is no blessing for regressing what was given from high,

When the agreement it was made, he put the sign in the sky,

It gets perverted not converted I see many conform,

The true battle for the soul means you have to perform,

Lesson learned or getting burned it's written down for the ones,

On hieroglyphs or in a cave as we prepare for the son,

You draw a weapon and keep stepping but our weapons are floored,

> *Our weapons are the love we have that keeps us*
> *all in accord,*
> *You see I'm ready for the struggle I won't loosen*
> *my grip,*
> *I see so many fall, and I ain't ready to slip,*

Appearing on Top of the Pops at the BBC studios in West London was a strange experience. We drove into the car park; I was thinking to myself that I have arrived. I felt so proud and thought, "this is two fingers up to the teacher that said I wouldn't amount to anything." It felt good to succeed and to know that I worked hard to get to this. I went into the reception area and was led to our changing rooms. There was lots of banging around outside the door, it sounded like a fight. When I looked out, it was the lead singer from Transvision Vamp racing up and down the corridor. We laughed as we joked that everyone would be expecting that from us. Nicky Campbell came into our room and introduced himself. He wanted to know what L.R.S stood for and then made up his mind to give us a full introduction. I felt relaxed although I thought it was going to be better than this. We went to the stage area and were met by the technical engineers. They handed us our microphones, and as I tried to turn them on, they reminded me that they are replicas. We went out to the main studio and there were more technicians it felt than people. My image of this day was slowly deteriorating quicker than I could form a positive vibe. The compere gave instructions to the crowd and rehearsed screams that were enhanced by a sound CD. I remember thinking 'just let us rap, this is what I do'. I was used to performing live, getting the crowd hype by entertaining from start to finish, but this was a different world. Nicky Campbell introduced us as D-Mob featuring the London Rhyme Syndicate, it was the best thing about the whole experience, getting our name out. The crowd screamed as they did the whole way through. As I left the studios, I remember standing in the car park and saying I'd be happy if I didn't return. I needed to get back to why I picked up the microphone in the first place. My value was to be real and miming felt fake to me. I started out wanting to make a difference and be a voice, that was my passion. Now I was being swallowed by a pop culture that still had issues with embracing diversity and rewarding it equally.

> *We've been blinded, I'm reminded of the words that I heard,*
> *Knowledge of self in a verb, so many kick to the curb,*
> *Look how we started we've departed from the essence of truth,*
> *Retrace the steps of our fathers with no bodies of proof,*
> *The argument it still remains why are we hated so much,*
> *From the land that we was promised to getting shot by the plod,*

> *It's out of order and we ought to just return to the*
> *Lord,*
> *To see a generation rise before the great lion roars,*
> *Self-respect respect yourself so many living to die,*
> *To know the meaning of the life pursuit I'm willing to*
> *try,*
> *We be using not abusing on the mic, word life,*
> *So I'm refusing what they doing till you see the light,*
> *With the ability lyrically we get ready to bless,*
> *We bring the focus of the protest with the truth no less,*
> *Open my eyes to all the lies that they've been saying for*
> *years,*
> *When the truth is told we won't be living in fear,*

Running parallel with 'It is Time to Get Funky' was the B.R.O.T.H.E.R Movement. B.R.O.T.H.E.R stood for Black Rhymes Organisation To Help Equal Rights. The B.R.O.T.H.E.R Movement was a collection of some of the most talented UK hip hop artists around in 1989. Instigated by a group from Brixton called Gatecrash, the main purpose was to raise awareness of the racial inequalities of the South African apartheid regime. The strong message in the music drew a parallel between the black struggle in South Africa and our own here in Britain. Assembling an all-star line-up, including the late Bernie Grant MP, each of the separate groups had the task of tackling the specifics of the Botha regime. The original aim of the organization was not only to raise awareness in South Africa but also to foster brotherhood where their existed hostility in the UK rap scene. All the artists' royalties were donated to the ANC. The single was called, 'Beyond the 16th Parallel'. The roster was a who's who of UK hip hop. It was the London Rhyme Syndicate, Overlord X, London Posse, Cookie Crew, Freshki, Demon Boyz, Gatecrash, Ice Pick, She Rockers, Junior San, MC Mello, Standing Ovation, Trouble & Bass, Hijack and Bernie Grant MP. This collaboration filled me with pride. It was also a time to get acquainted with people on a similar journey to my own. We were able to share stories and connect on a professional level.

The relationship between storytelling in the village and hip hop is one in the same. Rappers are modern-day storytellers. I used my lyrics to inspire the listeners, exposing them to a different view. I knew if we all came together, it represented a much more powerful entity than being separate. That was the beauty behind the B.R.O.T.H.E.R. Movement. Whatever your background, we all have common goals. It is our individual duty to smash the barriers placed in between us so we can achieve our potential and continue to advance as one people. I dreamed of using my voice to challenge the status quo through current events and personal narratives, and I was doing it. I wanted my audience to enjoy my music, but I also wanted it to make a difference in their lives. I wanted people to think when they listen to my music, not just get high and freak out on the dance floor. It was all about creating awareness and imparting knowledge. I was driven by the principle that social change came through knowledge of self and personal discovery. I wanted to reflect and transmit the truth and expose the attitudes that existed within mainstream culture. Instead of boasting or telling violent tales, I wanted to use rap as an innovative instrument against the opposing force of racism in England. I realised that nothing has meaning except the meaning I give it. I need to live my story, not the story others would ascribe to me. I choose my story; I choose to be what I believe.

Chapter 5
Making a difference

"We can choose to be affected by the world or we can choose to affect the world."

Heidi Wills

Our lives can be measured by the difference we make in another person's life. What's happened to the expression that bears witness? The arrival of Public Enemy challenged the young minds that they could be more than sports stars or gangsters. I was ready to take up the challenge; young black men began to wear African pendants as they desired to identify with their roots, influenced by groups like the Jungle Brothers. They wore African symbols and kente cloth. Hip hop was rapidly becoming the music for young people of all cultures.

"From a grimy and gritty life, I spit the bars you like.

Some brothers say its hype and freeze when I'm on the

mic.

I've loved this hip hop thing from day one blood.

It was me hitting the greens with the brandy in the

clubs.

We had the gual dem on lock, while the man dem with

their glocks.

More time in the dance you hear the matics go pop.

It all added to the vibes it made us what we was.

Hip hops first generation in the UK cuz.

Trying to make a raise, because a brother needs to eat.

Not qualified to be a lawyer, slinging herbs on the

streets.

Crime my sparring we knew no other way.

We had to seize our moment or watch it pass away.

Like soldiers, we face odds that were stacked up.

They tried to back us up, over loops we smacked it up.

Bringing something like you never heard before.

This yout man deh was vex and ready to get raw".

> "We came from those concrete cages where young hearts rage, all the way to the country's biggest stages. From the streets that cause fear, panic and mistrust, to modern-day poets that bring joy to the unjust."
>
> **REYNOLDS**

We had an avenue to express ourselves and get paid for it. Too many young males only had violence as their outlet. I saw too many friends die for nothing but the pursuit of the unreachable goal of financial freedom. Some were killed by young men who looked just like them. Young men with the same hopes and fears. Some were killed for drugs, one died from his close friend who was high on crack and stabbed him over a piece of KFC chicken. Life is too short on the block. Too many live fast and die young and we seem to act like that is okay. Every day we would be reminded of the choice we were making and the unique privilege we had.

"It's not what abilities you have that makes a difference it's what you do with these abilities that's paramount."

Byron Pulsifer

One of the biggest challenges in society for young people is to establish a voice. Through hip hop, we had a platform that gave us an outlet. From artists like Chuck D, Tupac, NWA, BDP, Eric B and Rakim, they said what we wanted to say. Young people across the globe identified with hip hop, setting trends that they could aspire to not only follow, but trends they could also replicate. These young rappers became forerunners in fashion and some even took the lead in awakening a generation to their responsibility as young people. In warehouses, parks or whatever venue would allow two turntables and a mixer, we all represented our tribes. Black or white, it was hip hop first, that was our culture. We had the London Posse, Hijack, Cookie Crew and MC Mello from South London, the Demon Boyz, Sindecut and Blade from North London, MC Duke, Overlord X from East London and London Rhyme Syndicate, Cash Crew and She Rockers from West London.

Questlove wrote, *"I urge and challenge musicians and artists alike to push themselves to be a voice of the times that we live in … I really apply this challenge to ALL artists. We need new Dylans. New Public Enemys. New Simones."* He went on, *"Songs with spirit in them. Songs with solutions. Songs with questions. Protest songs don't have to be boring or non danceable or ready made for the next Olympics. They just have to speak truth."*

Throughout the nineties, hip hop influenced as it has influenced all genres of music and became a leading voice in youth culture. This culture shows by example what adult culture should be as it embraces what it likes without excuse. They remove the ancient boundaries set by the fearful. We knew and believed that our colour defined beauty, it did not define a threat. This shows up the relics who desire segregation. In times past, division was used to rape a continent, and today, postcodes do the same.

"I used to hate the police but now they don't worry me.

What's gonna stop one of you from shanking me.

Different postcodes, kid I'm an African.

Via Jamaica with an English accent.

Free world we enter to fulfil.

Cities shake before the end many will.

Nobody moves, everyone's silent.

I learnt well on the shoulders of giants.

A lyricist with linguistics for the unjust.

From the one you trust, that's how I bust.

360 degrees in operation.

Like an addict to the sweet sensation.

Contagious, it means you can catch this.

You'll need more than DNA just to track this.

Try and crack this you know I ain't the one.

Free worlds on a roll and you think say we done".

It was during this time I realised that I would not quit. No matter how hard I had to work, I was going to chase my dream. I still got the buzz performing, so for me it was a no brainer. We still faced discrimination in employment and in the dissemination of opportunities. I still had a cause and there was no time to pause from the mission I had assigned myself. Pioneers like Chuck D and KRS ONE continued to deliver cutting-edge poetry for the advancement of global youth culture. Why should I be any different?

"You think say me done, me just ah come son.

40 years of wisdom wrapped up in this one.

300 years on and still we struggle on.

Fighting for my future and still I'm gonna keep on.

Using the mic like a leader, street preacher.

The innovator to inspire new leaders.

I won't deceive yer, like many did before.

Don't you know that I've been doing this since 1984?

> LRS stable Harlesden was my endz.
>
> Bregdrin had our backs when it was time to defend.
>
> It was always a struggle that's why so many hustle.
>
> Renew your intellect and use that kind of muscle.
>
> Sacrifices made I know my father made.
>
> I know my mother made for my path to be laid.
>
> You don't recognise, so you show no respect.
>
> Look your brother in the eye then shank him in the neck".

I needed things to happen, I had a thirst for adventure and these experiences fuelled my rhymes. It kept me in touch with what was current and what moved the crowds. I thought a record deal was the answer. Sometimes you must trust your creativity and take it where you're loved. If that means you sell from the boot of your car, then so be it. Most entrepreneurs understand that your brand is what people are saying about you. It was my goal to fuel that conversation.

"The freedom songs are playing a strong and vital role in our struggle. They give the people new courage and a sense of unity. I think they keep alive a faith, a radiant hope, in the future, particularly in our most trying hours."

Martin Luther King Jr

Everyone said how good the tracks were and how hard-hitting the rhymes were. In the same breath, the AnR would say you need some softer tracks like MC Hammer, and I nearly snapped. It was always hard beats and rhymes for me. We had a meeting with our manager and Danny D. He just had a hit with ACIEED but the media had turned on him as they said it promoted drug taking. He wanted us to give D-Mob a response. He had a backing track he had been working on and he gave it to us to write to. We went to Prince's pad and while we ate Frosties and smoked some weed, 'It is Time to Get Funky' was born. The concept behind the track was that the scene was sick, and we had the cure. In fact, we were the cure. When it came time to film the video, it was all based around a hospital. It was a light-hearted dig at the media who criticized D-Mob for the earlier track. It was a rollercoaster time of meetings, interviews and photoshoots. I released so much of my frustration in verse at that time; it was a dynamic outlet for me. I wouldn't change it for anything.

> *"It's how the free world is doing it.*
> *We knew we could, speech is clear when where moving in.*
> *An overcomer, always in my baggy jeans.*
> *Like a soldier, I know the routine and the scene.*
> *Radical the calling card of this fanatical.*
> *Drop the base with me that is compatible.*
> *Keep it real or else where gonna fade out.*
> *On the crossroads how many man selling out.*
> *The time will come, the time is already here.*
> *What matters most when I come I will not fear.*

> *Windrush I know the sacrifices made.*
>
> *Should I forget be like an aneurysm in the brain.*
>
> *Storyteller got tell it like it really is.*
>
> *Fairy tales we gotta leave them for the kids.*
>
> *Young man you're my son's biggest threat.*
>
> *Awaken your mind cause I ain't done yet".*

Even after we decided to go our separate ways and pursue solo interests, I was still hungry for the stage. I still had something to say. I thought about reinventing myself and the best name to describe me was the Problem Child. I began to meet new producers and put a catalogue of tracks together. The Problem Child was the personification of the angry youth who would not go out quietly. One evening, I went to Singers wine bar with MC Eric, he had just released a track with Technotronic. Singers was a place where unsigned artists performed and industry people frequented on a regular basis so they could snap up the next big thing. On my way out, I bumped into a familiar face, it was Flakey C. I hadn't seen him since he got his break on the Rapologists single with Whiz Kid. We talked about where we were both at and it seemed we were both at a crossroads. We met up and went on to make some real hard-core jams. We made tomorrow's music today and many industry people didn't have the foresight to see it. Many a day was spent in the lab creating pictures that led to hip hop. The industry wanted commercial music and we offered up the opposite. We brought heart and intelligence in our music and we considered it a protest with style. Regardless of all the struggles I went through, I knew I wasn't done yet. They could try and manipulate me into doing something that did not represent my core values, but they couldn't snuff out my internal rhyme. My heart cry was still louder than their inactivity. We were on the cutting edge of something great in the UK, but greed and a lack of foresight slowed down its progress.

Too much of the same thing depreciates the value of it. It is our duty to find the music inside, whatever it may be. Then we must come to the forefront and challenge the mundane. We must recognize we are gifted and use it to make a difference wherever we can. Within every generation, an individual rises up and flies the flag of their predecessors and continues the on-going dialogue. Why am I here? What can I contribute? Genuine role models are a rare thing; they have been replaced by sports icons, film icons and music icons. We replaced solid character for sparkly talent and then make excuses about why they are making the headlines for the wrong reasons. The media plays an interesting role in this. They help turn an ordinary individual into something larger than life and then shoot holes in their character because they can't live up to the image that was set.

> *"Learn the lessons from ages.*
>
> *From the endz with the concrete cages.*
>
> *Read the pages to focus the rages.*
>
> *Life amazes you live it in stages".*

I needed to learn to read in order to develop my mental muscles and my only option was to become a student, a self-taught learner. If I don't keep learning, how will I keep on earning? Only then will I create a space for myself to play my music. It is usually during life's struggles that character is formed in us. Inspiration can come from almost anywhere and from anyone. It all depends on how you channel it and how you let it affect you. It should be used to fuel your dreams and give you that extra push needed to go beyond the status quo. I remember my brother telling me to beware when people say they know you because they are saying they know what is in you. Setting the level of how far you are going to go. How much you can grow. They know your limits, and by that, they limit you. I am without limits and my dreams begin outside the box. The box that contains so many within its confines limits creative growth. Whatever your box is, it's time that you break out of it.

I spent every Thursday night emceeing at the Wag Club on Wardour Street. Rapperattack Soundsystem kept the dancefloor grooving downstairs. Along with a stack of emcees, Soulski Jam, MC Bronx, we would entertain on the mic. It was something I looked forward to as it was a venue where I could try out new rhymes and flows. I always got a great reaction from the crowd, which caused me to stay in tune and relevant.

> *"Free world, for one night only,*
> *For the hip hop crew that know me,*
> *If you wanna move then show me,*
> *If you got the skills let em go see,*
> *To the upcoming movers and shakers,*

> *Poppers lockers and even the breakers,*
>
> *All takers bringing in a new vibe,*
>
> *On the inside shine for your own tribe,*
>
> *Making moves as I do this,*
>
> *On the dance floor your feet already knew this,*
>
> *X-Factor just like Malcolm,*
>
> *With a dream like a King and I'm back son,*
>
> *Another hype one, it's too strong,*
>
> *Gimmie that mic cause you know that I'm coming on,*
>
> *In my zone don't care if you follow me,*
>
> *Free world, for one night only."*

It was D-day; I had a choice to make, music with a hard-core message which I loved, or a more commercial flavour which offered no lyrical depth but could be financially rewarding. I wanted people to like what I did, however, my inner drive was to write rhymes that made a difference. I had values and being real was important to me. I called it timeless lines – no matter what era, it would still be relevant.

"The money always looks good", I thought. But it would damage our ever-growing underground reputation. Do what you love and the money will follow you. We got to be real, just like Cheryl Lynn sung. It was emotional, I thought about Malcolm X and the way he stood up for a cause he believed in. I had to remind myself about what drew me to hip hop. KRS said, "It's not about the salary, it's all about reality." The reality was that they were getting paid. For me, hip hop was all about storytelling and that is the way it was used in the early days. Young men would tell the world their story, highlighting the many intricate issues they were facing. They were opening our eyes to their struggle. It gave us hope that some shared similar struggles to our own. It spoke to my heart and I was moved to action, yet the fact remained a brother needs to eat.

If I ever lacked direction or struggled to find inspiration, I would remember the giants who went before me. Those who paved the way before me, that is where I would find my artistic roots and counteract the commercial softness that was trying to force us to change. It was like an infection of my heart, and the only remedy would be to apply the antibiotic which would be some truly inspirational hip hop. Even when they tempted me with the almighty pound that was often dangled like a carrot, I didn't want to play that role. I grew up watching the black and white minstrels and I was not going to do that dance. Each time, we came back a little wiser and stronger. As an artist, I was searching for a style that was me. I wanted to make a difference.

Chapter 6

I need your strength

"The world breaks everyone, and afterward, some are strong at the broken places."

Ernest Hemingway

"Forces beyond your control can take away everything you possess except one thing, your freedom to choose how you will respond to the situation."

Victor Frankl

Strength is something I have needed to stay on course. It has shown itself in many forms and sometimes in unexpected ways. Friends and family have always been reliable sources to lift me up. Sometimes it has been the words of encouragement of a stranger, an enthusiast who has been moved by my rhymes. Sometimes it was a crowd going crazy, almost living every word with you. The hugs of a loving mother who believed in me when it looked like it was a distant dream. Another source of strength was finally recognising my weaknesses and counteracting them. The shoulder to lean on when times were hard and the ways to succeed were clouded. We all have to navigate our way through, and even if it seems you're stuck in the maze, don't give up. Every time a door closed on me, I looked for an open window. At times, you have to be like liquid, able to adapt to whatever life throws at you.

Dealing with chaos, it don't make sense,
It's like being caged in by an electric fence,
Sometimes you feel alone, with nowhere to turn,
Who knows your pain as your emotions burn?
We live and learn but are we learning as we live,
Questioning YAHUAH cause of what someone did,
Our lives are best understood as you look back,
But each day we live them forwards and so many miss that.

Every journey is filled with both highs and lows and the true test of your character is how you walk in both. I had a decision to make, would I keep writing with the hope of more shows or let it go? I had a second wind, but would I be relevant now? Things had changed and so did the perceived needs of the community. Ralph Emerson said, *"What you do speaks so loud that I cannot hear what you say."* Is the chaos we see now with youth culture a result of the breakdown of the family or is it by design? With the breakdown of the family and fatherlessness widespread in society, what we see is a generation that is fearless, without respect and no sense of belonging. Young men are looking for role models outside the home as we see a lack of fathers stepping up to the plate and fulfilling their duty to their children. The result is that we see young men trying to prove their manhood by their pursuit of the opposite sex and what they are willing to do if they feel disrespected. Young women struggle for identity without a true father in their life to continually reassure them of their beauty and importance. I need to step up my game and be what I can be for my children. I need to provide them with a launch pad for their potential.

In the English language, if a woman loses her husband, she becomes a widow. If a man loses his wife, he becomes a widower. If a child loses their parents, they become orphans, but a parent that loses a child is given no name. The reason for this is our children were meant to outlive us. To those who have lost a child or cousin or friend, you are in my prayers. Today we see young people dying for respect, their postcode or fast money. I want to bring your attention to the hyphen, or the power of the hyphen. The hyphen is the line between your birth date and your death date. It is a line that represents what your life is. What will yours represent? Will you leave a legacy to inspire others or one to be forgotten? We have the power to choose. Where there is no vision, we die, when we have no future hope, we let our dreams fade.

We don't need to fulfil negative stereotypes and fit the profiles of death. It's time we mark out an alternative destiny that embraces success and happiness.

> *When you see me on the road, it means I'm back again,*
>
> *I'm skinning teeth, because I'm sweet with my whole life my friend,*
>
> *By the grave of my mum, it was hell back then,*
>
> *But I have hope so one day that we will ride again,*
>
> *Memories will never fade, that's how I'm managing,*
>
> *I see my kids growing up and I'm imagining,*
>
> *A better life inside my home, well it is happening,*
>
> *A good wife is the key to never panicking,*
>
> *I smile again, even in the tragedies,*
>
> *I keep going. like I'm on batteries,*
>
> *I'm looking out the window as I drive by,*
>
> *Looking at the poverty and I'm always asking why,*
>
> *I'm praying through so that I can break through,*
>
> *It's nothing new it's what my brave ancestors do,*
>
> *Seen it, done it, and doing it again,*
>
> *Needing his strength so I can maintain.*

Desire gave me the strength to chase after my dream. Desire was most evident when I made up my mind to go for it one hundred percent, all of me working together to develop and articulate how I felt. It helped me make my dream known from the inside out. You see it first before you can be it. This is what rhyming meant and means to me. It enabled me to overcome obstacles, being booed off stage, not being signed by a major record label and helped me see my future positively. You can look at every situation and discover the nuggets you can grow from, but if you don't learn from them and then apply what you learn, what's the point? Hunger for success has an energy of its own, an energy that is seen as you stay up all night seeing your future, as you put pen to paper. I knew if I got myself around people like that it would rub off on me. You can't fake it. That's precisely why some make it through even though the odds may have been stacked against them. It made me become transparent and it stripped away all the masks that I would wear and left what really was me. It forced me to be who I was for real, and not hide who I was becoming. Rather than taking a leap into my dream and immersing myself in it, at times, I found myself shrinking back. By holding onto your dreams, you keep alive the potential to blow a fresh wind into them. Sometimes struggle against incredible obstacles. It can feel like they are impossible to overcome. Amazingly, we often end up finding that we have the strength to break through the barrier. I had to reach my goals in life despite the hardships and conflicts that I faced on the way. Has anyone ever told you that you could not do something? That you are incapable of accomplishing a goal you set out to complete? How did you feel? What did you do? By focusing on and realizing our dreams, we give others the encouragement to pursue their own dreams. Observation is the first step to being able to identify what may be blocking your way. It's impossible to move something or learn to find your way around it if you don't know what you're looking for or where it is. Sometimes we just need to look forward and walk towards the ideal.

There is no better than adversity. Every defeat, every heartbreak, every loss, contains its own seed, its own lesson on how to improve your performance the next time.

Malcolm X

The fear of failure, even after you succeed, can cripple you. Desire must outweigh the fears. Acronym of fear: F false, E evidence, A appearing, R real. Before I could overcome my fears, I had to be aware of them. The fear of falling and loud noises are our only natural fears, every other is a learnt behaviour. My fear of failure was developed from my days of underachieving in school. My family told me I was brilliant, but my teachers always seemed to be lowering my ambition. I wasn't born with these fears;

they didn't stop me from achieving my goals in hip hop. Yet it felt like a continual bombardment. In society, every failure is front-page news. Celebrities are built up and then shot down if they stumble. We don't want to be the one who makes the headlines for the wrong reasons. The one who gets into trouble, to be the universal fuel for the negative narrative. I understood the power of word of mouth as it was the vehicle that carried our momentum as a hip hop group. Sadly, it seems the media get more hits from putting a dreamer back in their place. How dare they dream, they can live their dream and be successful. It seems the media are happier that these dream upstarts return to the status quo. There was a saying that 'punks jump up to get beat down'. I didn't want to be a punk and I didn't want to be beaten down. Your only option fear leaves you is to not do anything but what is expected. The climate of fear is the elephant in the room – the elephant in most rooms. It was time for me to change my focus. I had to focus on what I could be, not what my fears were dictating to me. At times, fear stopped me from stepping into new challenges as I felt I didn't have the experience for them. Yet nothing was stopping me from learning new skills, the specific skills needed for my new challenges. Nothing was stopping me from reading more or building networks with more experienced individuals. The more I learn, the more I recognise the false evidence. The more knowledge I acquire, the more ability I have to drown out the fear. I need to apply the strength my father applied when he launched out from Jamaica to England. Industries went to Jamaica to recruit, and when they came here, the streets were paved with hatred and mistrust. He faced his fear – it is what they did, it is who he was. The end goal, the vision drove him to be an overcomer. He overcame and so can I, he did it for me and I do it for mine.

"Once in motion I am able to move a little quicker.

The neural groove laid down, my rhyme the trigger.

If it's down to me I'm going to leave you dancing.

One direction and I'm advancing.

A little hook from a crook that you mistook.

Shaking yourself on the dance floor take a look.

A young guy no not a juvenile.

Served my time, meanwhile my profile.

Love positive energy, a pacifist you wish.

I'm too powerful to let my fears dismiss."

I was inspired to use the stories of others who had to overcome. The visionaries who saw more than they had experienced, who transformed our todays by the sacrifices they made. My reality can't define my dreams, it is my dreams that must define my reality.

Without a dream would MLK have walked the walk he walked?

Talk what he talked, stayed on track when the road forked,

Even when the feds stalked, he stayed true to his hearts works,

What is our response to life even when life hurts?

My mum and dad both passed, still I'm not alone,

At times I feel I'm carried right into the end zone,

I'm heading home, and it feels like a major test,

Watch how I've grown and yeah I'm going to do my best,

Grief is a pain that one day we all face,

I choose where I find my place, peace at a steady pace,

A source of strength that you never knew you had,

Need when times are bad, keeping calm when you're really mad,

No times for fads, it's reviving the aching heart,

Ripped apart, pain in the chest fired from a dart,

We must be smart, there's no sitting on the fence.

I need your strength.

Sometimes people just get lucky. They are in the right place at the right time with the right mind-set. Most of the time, however, it isn't luck that makes the difference; rather, it is the fact they will not throw the towel in, in spite of the odds, failures, criticism or past mistakes. Much of the success of those I admire today is based on their refusal to stay defeated or give up. Thomas Edison failed more than 3,000 times in his attempts before successfully creating the electric light bulb. When asked why he persisted after so many failures, he replied that he hadn't failed, rather he had "discovered 3,500 ways not to make a light bulb." He used each failure as a learning experience and catalyst for the next attempt. To taste success, I had to continue to push forward, to strive to reach my goal. Discouragement, setbacks or losses are like weights trying to burden you. I had to keep faith with my purpose and stay on course.

To critique is so much easier than being a creative, theirs is not the way of vulnerability. When have you ever seen a statue dedicated to a critic? The world is full of people who are more than willing to tell you all the reasons why you can't follow your dreams or succeed at something others haven't done. Vision is about creating something new, not in contempt for the past, but built upon the foundation of the past and the present, emerging with a reality that is better than that which is currently available. When fully enacted, vision brings us closer to our ideals. The key question we ask is, "What do they really know about what I'm capable of doing?" You will never know unless you step into the arena. It's not enough to watch the game, it's not enough to get dressed for the game, as it is when you enter the field of play. When your kit gets dirty and you have perspired and put the work in, you are able to speak of what it's like in the arena.

Don't be putting up a fight, come into the light,

We be the ones that are shining bright,

Every thought will ignite, no hype to excite,

Creating insight, as I move in tonight,

If it's tasty then bite, strong on the mic,

Day light is coming for the ones in the night,

Sight over sight let me soar like a kite,

.When I say Yahusha walks, I know that I'm right,

Still too many rules, treated like fools,

We gotta know His plan; he's left us the tools,

His death brings it home and it's up to you,

Heaven's hittin earth as YAHUAH enters you,

Gotta go to church, wait, be the gathering for real,

Led by His Ruach not emotional appeals,

His grace gives me room to love so much,

I need your strength and your tender touch.

I remember walking through a cemetery and I began looking at the gravestones. The ages were so diverse, from babies and children to the elderly. I began to think about how much potential is lost in this place. How many unfulfilled dreams are lost in here? How many died without finding their music? How many lived trying to be something they're not, someone they're not? How much potential is locked away in prison? How many dreams are lost in a cycle of drug addiction and alcohol? Our dreams are so precious that we should not let anything get in the way of seeing them realised. As I look back on the whole process, for me to write, it was the merging of many random thoughts that produced an idea that caused a line. Leaving a positive mark was always the foundation that I chose to build on.

Injustice is a passion of mine; I hated injustice and wanted to speak out against it every time I had an opportunity. I would be a voice for those whose voice is not loud enough or whose voice is ignored. I wanted to be an arm to those who lacked the strength to initiate change in their situation. I wanted to make a difference where it mattered. Today, as I look out into society, too many young men are dying for a cause they feel is worth dying for, but in years to come, it will be forgotten. They die over a postcode and some are willing to kill over a postcode they will probably change when they are older. It makes no sense as I look back.

For me it is essential, I got to fulfil potential.

Got to be what I believe, anything else for real I got to leave.

I'm never ever gonna quit,

I'm gonna work hard so you best believe it.

I never gave up trying to fulfil my potential. I chased after it like my life depended on it. You should do the same. The difference between winning and losing is the choice not to quit. No retreat and no surrender, throwing the towel in must never be an option.

Different times I can remember how I have been strengthened by close friends and family. At times when I felt no one understood and no one believed in me, a gentle reminder from my friends and family supported my dream. They gave me energy to continue when I didn't have any. When I was faced with disappointments, it was their words that gave me that little bit extra to continue to fight. Their presence at some real hostile places, their support when things didn't go as we planned, helped me to get through some difficult times. It's not these times that could derail me, but how I respond to them.

As I glanced over my shoulder, I see the making of a man in the process of the making of a rhyme. I see the mind of a young man that trusted in the wrong things, becoming aware of the dangers of being naive. I see a young man step up to the plate to take his innings and drop verses for his generation.

Start by doing what's necessary; then do what's possible;

and suddenly you are doing the impossible.

Francis of Assisi

Being able to see beyond my current situation was key for me to move beyond my circumstances. Society told me I could only go so far, but I could see beyond what they saw for me. This is my dream, my passion, my gifting, all of them clues to the why of my existence. When I discover my passion, I discover my direction. I understand where I fit within the bigger picture. I understand my part in the bigger story, I find my music. Something is stirring inside of me, I need to allow it to come out. In the past, I may have squashed it, but not this time.

Chapter 7
Shine your light

"Shine your light and make a positive impact on the world; there is nothing so honourable as helping improve the lives of others."

Roy T Bennett

It was my time to shine, the act before me was going into their last verse. This was our big break; opening set for KRS One, the venue is the Thekla in Bristol. The Thekla is a cargo boat and stationed in the Mud Dock area of Bristol's Floating Harbour. Was this a coincidence that at the point where slaves were brought into England was now the venue for the children of slaves to entertain? KRS was one of my favourite rappers, but this time, I wanted to outdo him. The night before we were the opening act of three, KRS liked our set and asked if we could go just before them. I sat in the dressing room in silence; I was focusing on what I had to do. I was going through the perfect set again and again.

I was born with music inside me. Music was one of my parts. Like my ribs, my kidneys, my liver, my heart. Like my blood. It was a force already within me when I arrived on the scene. It was a necessity for me-like food or water.

Ray Charles

I developed my pre-show routine, first I envisaged the entire routine. This was the time I mentally and emotionally focused on what I had to do. It was at this point that I would let go of all that was happening at home or situations that were causing me stress. It was time to forget the traffic and connect with the story that I was about to tell. People come out to have a good time and forget their troubles. Tonight, I was going to be the instrument they would use. I had my performance clothes; I treated it like my work clothes. My outfit was all part of the show that I was going to perform. The door knocks and we get the 5-minute shout. My pace quickened as I paced back-and-forth backstage. I peeked through the curtains at the hungry crowd with anticipation in their eyes. The sound crew asked me if I was ready. I nodded. My mind was focused on the walk onto the stage to when I was holding the microphone. My heartbeat and breathing had become more pronounced. The sound man's voice trailed off as he signaled to the sound booth. I wiped the sweat off my hands for what seemed like the thousandth time. David had a confident look on his face. We were going to be fine; we had rehearsed this a thousand times. We could do this in our sleep. Hearing the excitement in the audience only fed into the excitement I was already feeling. 'You nervous?' I smiled at Prinz as I shook my head. My feet were restless, I checked my trainers. I straightened my tracksuit. David made his way to the turntables as the host walked towards the microphone. The introduction was a blur, I was too busy going through the performance in my mind. Stepping out onto the stage, lights, the screams of the crowd, the big sounds, then the silence, your heart is beating into your chest, and you feel your heartbeat, your stomach in your throat, and your mind recalling the lyrics from my first verse. That's what it was like for as I stepped out onto the stage. It was a total adrenaline rush, a natural high. For some shows it felt like home, i felt safe, it was my safe space to be my true self. Being on stage is more than a feeling, it allowed me to play my music on the inside and out. Having a connection with the audience is what makes each show special. When the audience are up for it, you know it's going to be a great night. Those closest to the stage we're screaming and shouting, they're energy fed me as my energy fed them, it was the perfect equation.

The venue was packed, the boat moving with the water, back and forth like a metronome. The ceiling was low and wet, the crowd waiting to be rocked. The MC introduced us and the crowd went crazy. I strolled out confidently and all I could smell was the water. Our backing track started to play and I started my verse. As I flowed, I moved from side to side, I was feeling this. I looked up and the whole crowd bar none were moving with me. A human metronome causing the whole crowd to move with me and, in turn, the whole boat rocked. For the thirty minutes the set lasted, this was the peak of my climb. I left the stage so pumped up. It got even better when KRS called us out for his finale – yeah, I was shining. Top of the Pops had nothing on this. After the show, we all went out to eat. KRS didn't say much but he did say, "You guys are dope. I loved what you guys did tonight; you gotta come to the Bronx." "For real? I'd love to." He was no longer this hip hop icon, he was my peer. We touched fists and then the conversation drifted back to what it usually did. The girls in the crowd, we could spot the needle in the haystack like we had a sixth sense.

We are not accidents put here by chance. We are here by design and each of us have unique gifts. Like small pieces of a puzzle, when we come together, our creative gifts create a beautiful tapestry. I had to remind myself that I am gifted and the biggest limiting belief I face is that I'm lacking something. Going on stage put those beliefs to the test, I had to learn to listen to a new narrative. Otherwise, I think I would have given up after the first setback. That is what made the show with KRS so special, we had to earn it through hard work and thought.

"Every time I thought I was being rejected from something good, I was actually being re-directed to something better."
Steve Maraboli

This broken world has taken from us, damaged us, but we can be restored. Now the battle is on, to live the life we were designed to live. We are made to function as human beings, not human doings having our identity attacked again and again and again. We are force-fed what beauty must look like, on the screen and in print. We are force-fed what success looks like, we are force-fed what it takes to be accepted. All the while, your identity is being stripped away. These limiting beliefs get stronger as our self-worth is limited. Some may suffer rejection due to their culture or social-economic standing. Like a frog in boiling water, we become less of what we were created to be. It's a trap, we are not free to be, this broken world values the doers. They want our identity in what we do, not who we are. I'm a teacher, a rapper, doctor or lawyer. The foundation is not stable, we are more than that. People only saw a snippet of my potential on stage, but it was a great starting point. We buy into the limiting theology as we limit ourselves and others to what they do or don't do. Inside we have an aching, we know there's something more. We know we are not satisfied but we are afraid to share our heart's desire because, if that is limited, we have nothing. We hide our dreams deep within and slog away day to day, losing ourselves in the process. We need to remember who we are. This broken world is always asking questions that limit us, but we are destined for more. We are more than we have been conditioned to feel, we are those who bring value to others and the tribes we belong to. Even though it's broken, we don't need to buy into its brokenness but our calling is to be who we are, ourselves. Bring value wherever you are. If this broken world has you twisted, don't give up or give in. It's in you, it's in all of us. Our creator left a little bit of him in each of us. This light must shine through our creative gifting. It's not what happens to us, but our response to what happens to us that hurts us. But today we understand who we are and what we are created to be: dynamic, powerful, and beautiful. It's a choice, it's always a choice. I have a light inside; I was made to shine!

My friends often told me that I would shine with the microphone in my hand; I was in my element. Some people are called to teach, some to play sport, some to act. I was skilled in verse. We are all destined for something and part of the journey we are on is discovering our life calling. We all have a skill set we have been blessed with. Many never get the backing needed to ride the storms and deal with the failures they suffer along the way. Failure is a stepping stone to success. I always take inspiration from people who use failure as a launch pad to succeed. We weren't made to hide our gifts; we are the crown of creation, we are designed to shine. My talent is YAHUAH's gift to me and how I use it is my gift to YAHUAH. The things we are passionate about are not random, they are our music inside.

"Shine your light, shine it bright.

Gonna get hype, gonna get hype.

In the darkness watch us glow.

When trouble comes watch us grow.

Watch my flow, watch it watch it.

Unu listen but you can't de-code it.

Standing firm like a pillar.

Wisdom winner strength I figure.

Free world, do you wanna enter?

In the centre, Spiritual mentor.

Gonna breath till theirs no breath left.

Gonna step from the rep with a clean intellect.

It be the Free world keep it in check.

I'm gonna shine bright no time left.

Wanna get hype, wanna get hype.

Out of the darkness into the light".

I realised that we had to leave a trail so others can follow. When I was a kid and they asked me what I wanted to be, my answer could have been anything from an Astronaut to a Footballer. Today, there is a poverty of aspiration and this generation has been let down. In the shadow of greed, you will always find poverty. I strived to succeed, but true success would mean that my children are fulfilling their dreams. It was time to pass on the baton to inspire a generation to be all they could be. It was time to transfer what I got from those who went before me; I had to transmit the vision from my heart to my verse. I had spent my time as a rhymer inspiring people I didn't know. I would perform to the best of my ability so they could enjoy the night's festivities. I wanted the DJs to play my songs; I wanted them to be appreciated. Now I wanted to leave a mark on people, like a branding iron. I wanted to leave an imprint upon the hearts of those who heard me.

> *"Outta sight and outta the night.*
> *Gotta aim high gotta get hype.*
> *Gotta get by gotta let fly.*
> *Gotta earn it not gonna get a bligh.*

> *And work it too.*
>
> *Bring what you got what you got bring it through.*
>
> *I'm never ever gonna fade.*
>
> *Show what you got and then get it laid.*
>
> *You gotta show your potential.*
>
> *Customize it come with the essentials.*
>
> *It's gonna take heart.*
>
> *Releasing your gift is kind of an art.*
>
> *The right kind of start with the right kind of flow.*
>
> *Gives the right kind of glow from the right kind of pro.*
>
> *It's time to ignite.*
>
> *Shine your light".*

To make it in life, talent is not enough. You've got to have the character and work ethic to back it up. Every day, even when encouragement is not forthcoming, you have to keep going. When the odds are stacked against you, don't give up. If you do your best, then that is good enough.

> *"Time to release and increase the tempo.*
>
> *Do what you do best, then you got to let go.*
>
> *To the get go, got to get yours.*
>
> *No matter how hard leave it all on the floor.*
>
> *We all got talent.*
>
> *Don't hold back make something happen?*
>
> *Find the strength from within.*
>
> *It's where your gift dwells and where you begin.*
>
> *Never stop at you can't.*
>
> *Never say no like a seed I got to plant.*
>
> *It's like a race and you got to hit the line.*
>
> *No time for a negative style.*
>
> *The sign is a mind that is active.*
>
> *Active to get it on so step to the positive.*
>
> *Crew you once knew on a dope tip.*
>
> *Still on a dope tip, so now you want to get with it".*

On May 29, 1953, Sir Edmund Hillary was the first man to climb to the summit of Mt. Everest. At 29,035 feet, you are at the tallest point on earth. However, he didn't achieve this accomplishment in his first attempt. In fact, in 1952, a few weeks after a failed attempt, he was addressing a group of people in England. During his talk, he walked to the edge of the platform, made a fist and pointed at a picture of the mountain. He said in a loud voice, "Mount Everest, you beat me the first time, but I'll beat you the next time because you've grown all you are going to grow... but I'm still growing!" He knew that his personal growth of knowledge and skill would inevitably lead to overcoming the mountain itself. How high can you climb? Have you ever considered the fact that everything ever accomplished once held the title, 'never been done'? One of the reasons I love sports so much is that world records are set all the time. When a new record is set, somebody raises the standard. At times, we worked so hard not to let our own limitations dictate to us. The past doesn't need to determine who you are or what you can do. You are still here, and while you have breath in you, there is hope.

Your past failures do not make you personally a failure, they are just stepping stones. In fact, it's often said, "The road of success is paved with failure." Everything ever invented, every record ever set, every problem ever solved was by somebody who decided that the 'impossible' is 'possible'. Don't let what others say or do limit you. Somebody needs to be the first. Why not you? Why not now? See the end, invite your imagination into the process. See it, believe it, then you can work towards it. Consider the words of Gentleman Jim Corbett:

"Fight one more round. When your feet are so tired that you have to shuffle back to the center of the ring, fight one more round. When your arms are so tired that you can hardly lift your hands to come on guard, fight one more round. When your nose is bleeding and your eyes are black and you are so tired that you wish that your opponent would crack you one on the jaw and put you to sleep, fight one more round – remembering that the man who always fights one more round is never whipped."

I hope for real that you're listening,

Pause for a moment till you see what we bringing in,

Keep fighting hard, my heels I be digging in,

Until they let me in the effort I be putting in,

My thoughts are sending in, that's the way that I begin,

The penny drops in the mind before I'm finishing,

I'm never quitting my backs against the wall man,

Bust a rope a dope like Ali against Foreman,

Ready to rumble gloves on, stay humble,

When the bell rings stay true never crumble,

Float like a butterfly sting like a bumble,

Fight another round kid stay stumble,

It burns like fire with flames as I hit,

My life fighting can't you tell that I'm fighting fit,

So many suffer and their dying from it,

Don't hide your face at times where going to be hit,

Through the pain that I feel I keep going,

The more I learn the more I know, I keep growing,

My vision is the seed, I keep sowing,

Sometimes I go against the flow to keep flowing,

> *Counter punch from the ropes cause now I'm living my dream,*
>
> *I won't be dropping my hands, I've come to far to give in,*
>
> *The opposition is ruthless, hitting hard but he's toothless,*
>
> *Every battle you face without heart is useless,*
>
> *So fight another round fight on higher ground,*
>
> *Just rise to your feet we can never stay down,*

There have been many times that I have thought about giving up and assigning my dreams to remain as dreams. But I have been inspired to fire at various times in my life. This quote always gives me strength and focus to shine my light. It's not in my DNA to quit. Always remember that if you don't give up, you're still in the game. This resonated with me and in me.

Inner strength may demise so don't be surprised,

Got that look in your eyes as it attacks your mind,

It's time for showing your spine, we know its serious

times,

It's awakening mine, it's not the end of the line,

Every angle is blocked, I got the key to unlock,

Sometimes your skill is not the reason why you're

getting the knocks,

It's all coming on top, I don't think it will stop,

Allow your passion to push you, then all the locks will

pop,

So, fight another round you've come too far to quit,

Keep reaching for your dream, reach out for it.

"Someone in your ancestral line survived being chained to other human bodies for several months in the bottom of a disease infested ship during the middle passage, lost their language, customs and traditions, picked up the English language as best they could while working for free from sun up to sundown as they watched babies sold out of the

arms of their mothers and women raped by ruthless slave owners.

Given first names but no last names, no birth certificates, no heritage of any kind, braved the Underground Railroad, survived the civil war to enter into sharecropping. Learned to read and write out of sheer determination. Faced the cross burnings of the kkk, reverted their eyes from the black bodies swinging from the trees. Fought in world wars to return to America as boys, marched in Birmingham, hosed in Selma, jailed in Wilmington, assassinated in Memphis, segregated in the south, ghettoised in the north, ignored in history books, stereotyped in Hollywood, and in spite of it all someone in your family endured every era to make sure you would get here and you receive one rejection, face one obstacle, lose one friend, get overlooked and you want to quit? You will never know what it took to survive from generation to generation so you could succeed. Don't you dare let them down."

Author unknown

Men and women survived the horrors of slavery. Stripped of everything and yet still able to see beyond their condition and build towards a better future. True dreamers, despite their oppression, were able to dream of freedom. What price has been paid so that I could shine? I can't take it lightly, my freedom to choose has come at a price. I choose to be the best version of me and I'm willing to be changed in the process.

A man met a guru in the road. The man asked the guru -
'Which way should I go to achieve success?'
The robed, bearded sage said nothing, but he pointed to a
place in the distance.
The man, thrilled by the prospect of quick and easy
success, rushed in the appropriate direction. Suddenly,
there came a loud 'Splat.'
Soon, the man limped back, tattered and stunned,
assuming he must have misinterpreted the message. He
repeated his question to the guru. 'Which way should I go

to achieve success?' The guru again pointed silently in the same direction.

The man obediently walked off once more. This time the 'splat' was deafening. When the man crawled back, he was bloody, broken, tattered, and irate.

'I asked you which way I should go to achieve success,' he screamed at the guru.

'I followed the direction you gave me, and all I got was splatted! No more of this pointing! Talk!'

Only then did the guru speak. What he said was: 'Success is that way. Just a little past splat.'

Author Unknown

I opened my eyes, it was still dark and backstage was softly lit. My senses heightened; I was so pumped, everything else seemed like it was in slow motion. Something instinctively told me that I had to seize the moment, it was now or never. My heart felt like it was going to explode; it felt like everyone could hear it. Breathing in the cocktail of alcohol, perfumes and tobacco only strengthened my resolve. The building was animated, the ceiling sweating from the toxic atmosphere within. I looked at my Gucci timepiece and quickly straightened my clothes. It was organised chaos and I was its architect. The bass line was hypnotic, sending its hungry listeners into a trance. The music was building to a crescendo. This was my hour, the arena erupted into a near-deafening eruption of pure emotion.

Chapter 8
Free like that

"Freedom is being you without anyone's permission."
Anonymous

"The one thing you can't take away from me is the way I choose to respond to what you do to me. The last of one's freedoms is to choose one's attitude in any given circumstance."
Viktor E. Frankl

After many nights awake reading, I finally understood the world around me. For decades, the years of decadence and self-centred living have finally taken their toll. I had spoken about it and rapped about it. The years of compromise had finally had their effect, and like a snake lying in wait for its prey, I have finally bitten back. And now we have reached the moment of truth, the tipping point: either we wake up, stand up, speak up, and act up, or we run the risk of becoming irrelevant to those who need us most. Even with the great technological advances, we can so easily become a generation that repeats the mistakes of the previous generation. That is why this is a call to all creatives, to all those who desire to have a voice, to stand up. I was a father, so rhymes about material possessions and killing or girls were of no interest.

It was all about bringing wisdom. Since the early 1960s until today, divorce has only increased. Teen suicide has exploded and the age of those who have accepted this as a viable option is getting younger. Now, some are even making online pacts and have organised suicide groups. That is why the 'Message' by Melle Mel has even more relevance to this generation, 'it's like a jungle sometimes'. How sad that some children feel the world is better off without them. We all miss out, as their potential is never realised. We now have cyber bullies and cyber predators trying to exploit the vulnerable online.

Violent crime has gone through the roof, the prison population has outgrown the prisons, the percentage of babies born without stability has risen, and the end is not in sight. We have more families living in poverty and that is not acceptable or comfortable as I write this. The last generation's rebellion has become this generation's curse, what was unthinkable thirty years ago, today we live with and we have the daytime talk shows to prove it. We are desensitised to so much that would cause past generations to respond in protest and uproar. I have witnessed the innocence of children lost at lower ages at each governmental change.

We live in the age of self, with self-help books flooding the market; we are encouraged to go it alone. I started rapping to bring worlds together. I was seeing next-door neighbours so far apart, it was frightening. In a time of mistrust, the wedge of division is driven further between communities. Since 9/11 and 7/7, we have a new group to target our mistrust. In the 70s and 80s, it was the black communities. In the 90s, it was the Asian community, then it's Muslims, now it's those seeking asylum who are the target of our mistrust.

We cannot fall into the trap of acting as if we are the centre of the world. Just because we exist in separate bodies, with our own private thoughts and our own private feelings that nobody else can hear or sense. Just because this causes indifference in us to the needs and feelings of others, we can't remain like this without recognizing the connection we have with each other. It's the butterfly effect – a butterfly moving its wings on one side of the world causes a reaction that leads to an event on the other side of the planet. What we do affects others, and when we pursue our dreams, it strengthens others. I wasn't built to exist on my own; I have always felt the need to be a part of something.

My style, language and culture has often been described as street. It is where I found belonging and a sense of purpose. Hip hop gave me somewhere to go, something to do and we had pioneers to show us the way. But now my identity was on the line, my purpose, I needed something to live for. I have seen enough dreams and aspirations die, which leads to a loss of life. All I wanted was to be accepted for who I was. Society didn't recognise me, but the streets did. Hip hop gave me the GPS coordinates to navigate my way through. I watched as friends chased after street recognition in other ways. Some found belonging and validation in gangs. They found the stability and safety they weren't getting at home. They would protect their new-found family by any means. We felt the disaffection of the national curriculum, the aspiration killer. If we couldn't run fast, sing, rap, DJ or kick a ball, we felt compelled to become a street player. Hollywood glamorises it and rappers rapped about it, so it seemed like a viable option to get paid. With no support or return to a formal lifestyle, the informal lifestyle appealed and, suddenly, those who have been limited their whole lives feel powerful. We became the stereotype that an institutionally racist society feared. The line was drawn, this was who I was, it is what I identified with. This darkness cultivated my anger. Too many were in and out of prison. Live fast and die young seemed like a great way to go. I hated the system because I believed the system hated me. I was headed nowhere fast and I wanted out. We all desire to know who we are, what gifts we have and what we can contribute. Within a system that desires control, we stifle the very freewill that sets us apart from all of creation.

If my experience is to be defined by loneliness and separation, then I have failed in what I set out to achieve. That would mean my impact was incomplete, unsettled and unfulfilled, this could lead me to try and fill the holes in my life. This need may produce feelings of insecurity, and the desire to fill that hole with whatever will put an end to the pain. Some will try to silence the pain with whatever numbing agent is close at hand: alcohol or drugs, non-stop work, or a pattern of controlled behaviour. Others choose religion, it can be a very vulnerable time, you must be aware of being exploited. I had to realise that there was more going on than what I consciously recognised. Could this be the eternal struggle taking place? Was there a bigger picture, and if so, what was it?

When I studied slavery, it led me on a journey. A journey at times I didn't want to be on, one that I knew would impact me deeply. The injustice and ferocity of the greed struck at my heart. Why did this happen? Why am I still facing the worldview that, somehow, I am lesser due to my cultural heritage? The National Front had a chant, 'There ain't no black in the union jack'. Black men and women were the subject of vile abuse. I remember my mum telling me about a time she was on her way to work and a man asked her the time. Before she could respond, he said, 'time to go home, darky'. Football players were lambasted for doing their jobs, bananas were thrown onto the pitch, monkey chants from the stands. Cyril Regis was sent a bullet on his England call-up. I took their hate and it fired me up. I wrote a track called 'The Dancefloor Shakes'. The chorus was:

> *'There ain't no black in the union jack, there ain't no black in the union jack, there ain't no black in the union jack, so there ain't no way I'll stand under that.*

I thought that I would be happy if I had the nice house, nice car and all the fame. I watched my dad work so hard to put food on the table. We never lacked anything, but society promotes more, it advertises the latest. It makes you feel that somehow you're missing out if you don't have it. I would dream about how full it would make my life and the respect I would get. Material possessions can never fulfil the internal desires I had. I know a lot of wealthy people who are not happy. Their lives seem tortured, not happy with their looks, their families – they are just not content. I didn't catch on right away, but I soon came to the realization that happiness didn't come from the pursuit of material things. Happiness comes through the pursuit of finding your music, that very thing you was placed on the planet to fulfil. I had to know myself and love myself enough to pursue my dream. I had to treat myself like I would a friend. Whenever they struggled, I would encourage them to keep on and not give up. I would tell them they have what it takes. It was my time to do it for me. Yet I felt confused, the constant rejection through racism made it hard for me to manage my emotions. I battled with thoughts of revenge against racists, it was infecting me. I didn't like how I was feeling, I felt weakened by it. I wasn't sure how to overcome it, I was angry that society had found a way to distort my music. I felt powerless against the narrative that painted a picture of me and where I was from. All my experiences were coming together in a painful crescendo. I launched

183

myself into reading as much as I could. It shaped my understanding. In the beginning, it fuelled my anger, but it slowly drove me towards the truth. I was inspired by the strength of the slaves. How they maintained their dignity in the most horrendous of conditions. In all what was done to them, they held onto their free will to choose their attitude. I have no excuse; true freedom is knowing regardless of my circumstance I can choose my response; it is my power to choose. It was in my hands to speak the true narrative and paint a true picture.

"Violence is already active here; it is built into the very structure of the existing society. If we seek a world in which men do the least possible violence to each other (which is to state just the negative of it), then we are committed not simply to try to avoid violence ourselves, but to try to destroy patterns of violence which already exist."

Barbara Deming

I have always wanted the truth and now is no different. Sometimes I had to remind myself of the impact my rhymes have made to give me extra fuel on my journey. I would find encouragement through positive words. For me, I feel blessed that what started in my heart has now translated into an innumerable amount of hearts. Reaching further than a sole voice could travel, across the country and around the globe.

> *"Like a bird in the sky, I'm free like that.*
> *Uniquely created, I be like that.*
> *20 20 vision, I see like that.*
> *Cause I'm free like that, so I live like that.*
> *Loving money, is more addictive than crack.*
> *Loving things are more seductive than lack.*
> *We love things that don't love back.*
> *Desire runs deep and it's like that.*
> *Name brands, so many fast cars.*
> *Big ballers, ghetto superstars.*

> *Add a strap to desire like that.*
>
> *No ways to make a raise, kids gonna react.*
>
> *We been telling you for years about that.*
>
> *You choose to ignore it, while it stays black.*
>
> *I done tell you that I roll like that.*
>
> *I speak like that, cause I'm free like that".*

There seems to be a strategy to lull us to sleep until we lose our convictions and our sense of fight is gone. It is seeking to lure us into a form of living that has no power – it is more like existing. Fear cannot and should not shape us; fear cannot stop us singing that song that is burning in our hearts. If we don't take a stand now, if we don't rise and speak and act now, then instead of being liberated, we will see more innocent lives destroyed. Our society is deteriorating all around us, the question I ask is why? Have we been side-tracked and distracted by the love of materialism at the expense of our youth? As a result, we have not impacted our generation. We have fallen asleep and have lost the capacity to use our YAH given gifts. Rather than making a difference in our world, rather than being free, we are trapped. The world has made a difference in us.

Everyone who breathes, high and low, educated and ignorant, young and old, man and woman, has a mission, has a work. We are not sent into this world for nothing; we are not born at random; we are not here, that we may go to bed at night, and get up in the morning, work for our bread, eat and drink, laugh and joke, sin when we want, repent when we are tired of sinning, raise a family and die. God sees every one of us; He creates every soul for a purpose,

John Henry Newman

> *"So, keep your anger in check and control that.*
>
> *Daddies not around man he bailed like that.*
>
> *Never follow in his footsteps or replay that.*
>
> *Be a father to yours and man it up like that.*
>
> *It takes a man to raise a man, and I get that.*
>
> *Respect to the mothers who stand like that.*
>
> *They tuff it out in the ends and cover up the cracks.*
>
> *And still they get the blame for what the youth lacks.*
>
> *So many wanna blame and reframe the music.*
>
> *Take a look at how they live and see who's abusive.*
>
> *I see the anger in the youth and they're hitting this.*
>
> *So many missing this, youths are resisting this.*
>
> *When truth hits your heart, you'll be dissing this.*
>
> *Make you wonder what the Free world mission is.*
>
> *Can't you see that I roll like that?*
>
> *I speak like that, cause I'm free like that".*

What else should we do? Our presence must be felt. Shouldn't we make a difference? Are we not the writers of history? This is our moment, this is our time. If we free ourselves from the things that hold us back, from our lusts, addictions, and our obsessions, and give ourselves over to the purposes of YAHUAH, we can shake this nation. We are the history makers and world shakers, we who are prepared to rise above the status quo. The fire starters who need to spark the flame. The revolution began when people said, "Something is missing. Something is wrong. There must be something more than this." There must be something more than eating and drinking, working and sleeping. There must be something more than simply getting a good education so that you can find a good job and have a good family so that your kids can get a good education and find a good job and have a good family so that their kids can get a good education. There must be something more than the education taught to keep us from asking these questions. This was the spark that caused me to find my voice.

"Create something out of nothing and that's a fact.

Able to act at will, and I do that.

Stay free of all restraints, how are you liking that.

Freedom is a state and we're still finding that.

We need to live the truth, I believe in that.

Not popular opinion, we can't do that.

Political correctness, what is that?

Treat a man like a man, don't patronize like that.

So many stories that never get told.

Government make promises that never hit road.

They always flip the script like that.

Vote for frauds like that, that lie like that.

Success is not a given, we gotta plan like that.

If you aim at nothing, you're gonna hit that.

I be what I believe and I live like that.

For real like that, where free like that".

What is it to be free? Free from the opinions of others. Free from the limitations they place on you. Free from the expectations that people set and assume you can't go beyond. Free to be yourself without the fear of being ridiculed because you don't conform to their preconceived idea. Free from the stereotypes that have been enforced on us to keep us back. Free to be the best I can be. Within hip hop, I experienced a real sense of belonging. The restrictions that society placed on me were removed. It sparked a desire within me.

The spiritual path – is simply the journey of living our lives. Everyone is on a spiritual path; most people just don't know it.

Marianne Williamson

We are all on a journey, knowing or unknowing. Some are walking at a slow pace, others a little faster, and some are even running. It doesn't matter how fast you go, just as long as you are going and are making progress. Everything is a lesson and every lesson helps you take another step on your spiritual journey.

Every tree we see scale the heights of the horizon has one thing in common: deep roots. The invisible time spent reaching into the earth gives the tree the resilience to withstand the storms and adverse weather. What cannot be seen is forming the foundation for what is seen. The inner world creates the outer world. We celebrate the fruit, not the root, yet it's the root that allows us to develop the fruit. The more we learn and develop who we are means we position ourselves for greater success.

Chapter 9
You don't understand me

"Beware when someone says they know you. They don't know your potential or what you are capable of. We can't allow anyone to set a limit on our potential."

Reynolds

Ronnie Wilson, aka Flaky C, was different. He was my calm in the middle of the madness I was facing. He was around from the pioneering days of the UK hip hop movement. A chance meeting or divine appointment at Singers Wine bar led to a fantastic opportunity. We started working together and made beats and rhymes. I was changing from a rapper into a young man of destiny. At times, it felt like I was caught between two people: who I was and who I was becoming. I had no control of the things that happened outside of me, all I could control was how I responded. I looked at my life and wondered about the things I had seen and lived through. I thought about the way I reacted in outbursts of anger. I was angry about racism, the lack of black role models in the public sector, the hidden agenda to suppress a generation. My life messages had been formed throughout my childhood. My experiences shaped my understanding. In 1975, I went with my father to pick up my sister from the children's home she worked at. We arrived as a family was meeting a child, it was surreal. We would have to wait until the meeting had finished. I went into a playroom and sat with a young boy who was alone. He looked upset and told me that no family had come to take him. Even though he was very young, he felt that something about him was unlovable. This impacted me deeply and stirred up the advocate in me. Another life-shaping event I remember was a teacher saying to me before I left school that I wouldn't amount to anything. I was that child that always had a question. I didn't take what was said at face value and wanted to know more. His limiting belief about me stimulated my anger. The day after I appeared on 'Top of the Pops', I remembered his words. They said I talked too much and it was a negative, now it was a positive. I went back to school and took a signed copy of the record.

Another life-shaping experience happened around this time. I went to celebrate our success with friends at a wine bar in Notting Hill Gate, 'It is Time to Get Funky' was in the top ten of the national singles chart. I arrived early and was approached by two men. They accused me of selling drugs and wanted to search me. I explained I had just arrived for a celebration. He grabbed me and started to forcefully search me. I asked for his ID number, but he grabbed me and started punching me in the face as he frogmarched me into Notting Hill Gate police station opposite the wine bar. I was placed in a cell, and after 30 minutes, I was released. I was filled with a burning rage; I told the policeman on the desk. I can't wait for carnival. As a child growing up in the era of the Sus law, I had already developed a mistrust of the police. The Sus law meant they could stop and search anyone they determined suspicious. Many officers thought West Indian heritage was suspicious and disproportionally stopped young black youths. These experiences left a mark on me and had affected me at a heart level. Internally, I was confused and angry, I had become so defensive. I needed to know that I belonged and had something to offer. The National Front pushed their right-wing brand of hatred and they wanted to send all black people back to their countries of origin. I wanted and needed to know that I was valued, and I knew in my heart that I wasn't here. I wanted to know that my voice counted, and it didn't. I was at the tipping point. I had been reading about Malcolm X and was reminded of his journey. I began reading the Quran, but I didn't find any direction for my life within its pages or answers for my internal questions. I wanted something personal that would be real to me. I was reminded of the journey of the slaves. The horrors of the middle passage. The stripping away of their dignity, the lies created to justify it. The role of the church within the process.

Darkness cannot drive out darkness; only light can do that.

Hate cannot drive out hate; only love can do that.

Martin Luther King, Jr.

I read about Buddha and the New Age movement and they all left me feeling empty. I needed something that would define me, that would speak to my soul. I needed my silent voice to be heard. I needed to know that I could be forgiven as I was finding it tough to forgive myself. I was angry that my family tree was severed due to slavery. What about their history was so powerful that the colonialists have continually hidden it from existence? I needed to know that I was loved without condition.

I was introduced to hatred as I innocently grew. Within all my searching, it ended with the truth that YAHUAH is love. That night, I began to read: *"For I know the thoughts that I think towards you, says YAHUAH, thoughts of peace, and not of evil, to give you an expected end. Then shall ye call upon me, and ye shall go and pray unto me, and I will hearken unto you. And ye shall seek me, and find me, when ye shall search for me with all your heart. And I will be found of you says YAHUAH."*

It's like YAHUAH was speaking to me, it freaked me out so much that I closed the book. I thought 'wow, let me try again'. I opened and read, *"Before I formed you in the belly I knew you; and before you came forth out of the womb I sanctified you, and I ordained you a prophet unto the nations."*

It was like a light being switched on. YAHUAH was speaking to me, all my time struggling with identity. The deep-rooted mistrust I felt after I witnessed racism, the slave trade and the impact on my psyche. For the first time, I prayed for real. "YAHUAH if you are real, show me, show me that I might understand." I felt an overwhelming sensation followed by a feeling of peace. It felt like I was loved, I was worry-free at that moment. I sat meditating and a sense of peace flowed over me. It was then I sensed that if I wanted to know more, I had to read for myself. **I had to step outside of the** church structure in order to see and understand that there is indeed more truth. I didn't want someone between me and YAHUAH, now that I could access him for myself, it was just what I was going to do.

Love is the only force capable of transforming an enemy into friend.

Martin Luther King, Jr.

I prayed and consumed YAHUAH's word. I was already in the habit of reading and studying. I had previously experienced this in my awakening. I read about slavery as my search identity intensified. I had consumed books about the world faiths, and they led me to YAHUAH. As I consumed the word, I felt an overwhelming sense of His presence. I phoned Ronnie and told him I wanted to be baptised. Ronnie's friend, Malcolm (we called him Mouse), belonged to a gathering and they were having a baptism service that weekend. It was a spiritual experience for me. As I came out of the water, I spoke in a language I had never learned. I was buzzing, I knew what it felt like to be high and this was better than any high I had previously experienced.

That night, I dreamed that young people were falling into the abyss. It was like a human waterfall. I tried to reach out to grab some, but they slipped through my grasp. I woke up with a sense of despair and failing. It was an overwhelming amount of people. It was then I sensed a quiet voice, it said, "You must know me." My call would not be dependent on what I do but it would be dependent on who I am. YAHUAH said his departure would be more beneficial to us, as he was leaving us his Ruach Hakodesh. YAHUAH's Ruach is in me, changing me from glory to glory. Out of who I am, I will naturally do what he called me to do. Regardless of the limited beliefs I may stumble across, YAHUAH is more than enough. I soon realised YAHUAH had been showing me himself through my passion and desires. In my childhood, as a rapper, during my struggles with identity. He was there when racism reared its ugly head and he was there when I was filled with anger. He was present, and it was then I understood he was always present. At times, people focus on the outcome but fail to celebrate the journey.

"Some people come into our lives, leave footprints in our hearts and minds and we are never the same again."

Jared Leto

I don't consider myself a part of the modern-day church system. My desire was to know the creator and serve Him in Spirit and Truth. Everything in His creation is linked to His name, His character and His attributes. Everything in His creation esteems His name by the vibrations, noise or sound they make, yet I called Him by a name that would have been unrecognizable to his disciples. I believe that YAHUAH and His only brought-forth son, Yahusha, should be called by their true set-apart names, not by the titles Lord, God, or the mistranslated name of Jesus. I am simply telling my story to encourage those of you who may be on a similar journey, and to clarify why I use the terms YAHUAH and Yahusha for those of you who have questions about what I believe.

I haven't followed the traditional path. For me, it is a personal relationship through faith. Faith gives us hope and has the power to help us overcome fear. It gave me the resilience to deal with and overcome the negative stereotypes I had been saddled with. I found the church restrictive, they wanted me to fit in, not stand out. I found there was a difference between Yahusha and the rules the ministries I attended used. I didn't need religion to underpin my faith. Yahusha said true religion is looking out for widows and orphans. Yet, today, it is different organisations with differing beliefs asking you to buy into their brand of religion. They do what has always been done, I just wanted to know if it should be done. Religion reminds us at the expense of our faith that we need the ministry or leader in our lives. People show up every week and follow the same programs they did the week before; they go through the same motion and hope something changes. The fact is, nothing changes because of the program. It got in the way of my faith and the organisation felt too controlling. I didn't want to be neutralised at the expense of my creativity. I had been given a gift, and the very place I expected it to thrive, it nearly died. I was told I didn't need to rap as I could be something more. They denied my music so I could fit into their plan. I had to do what I believe in, not what someone else was saying for me to believe. My faith is my inner world, that is the foundation for my actions. When I stand on stage, when I put together an inspirational talk. It is what I impart through passion, my music inside. It forms who I am. I am not like anyone else. I was made to stand out, not in line.

"What, to the American slave, is your Fourth of July?
I answer: a day that reveals to him, more than all other
days in the year, the gross injustice and cruelty to which
he is the constant victim. To him, your celebration is a
sham; your boasted liberty, an unholy license; your
national greatness, swelling vanity; your sounds of
rejoicing are empty and heartless; your denunciation of
tyrants, brass-fronted impudence; your shouts of liberty
and equality, hollow mockery; your prayers and hymns,
your sermons and thanksgivings, with all your religious
parade and solemnity, mere bombast, fraud, deception,

impiety, and hypocrisy-a thin veil to cover up crimes
which would disgrace a nation of savages."
Frederick Douglass

I've tried many things that didn't work out for me, but I had no way of measuring the outcomes. Without my music inside to guide me, I could only try to fit in. All the time I separated what I do from what I loved, I remained chained to the status quo. I was reduced to writing rhymes in my car as I waited for my children to finish school. Feeling frustrated in my job as I dreamed about inspiring and entertaining on the greatest of stages. I made so many poor career-related choices during that time. But it didn't matter, I wasn't about to give up. I must have been a slow learner, but I got there in the end. I realised my music inside shows you who I am and it's how I impact the world around me. The invisible becomes visible as I release my music. My faith in YAHUAH inspires me to be my best self.

This world put so many conditions on me, from how I should look, the way I should talk, and how I should be. I was ready for change and I was open for the truth. I had become so complex, and by this point, no one understood me – I didn't understand myself. Flaky believed in YAHUAH and he never tried to persuade me or force me to be something. He wanted to see me free of the *internal* torment. He always encouraged me to ask YAHUAH to reveal himself, but I had to be open to receive the message. I had to tune in to the right frequency, for me, it was my desperation for truth. I knew there was more to my existence than I had experienced so far. I refused to settle for the status quo, for anger, hatred and regret. I asked myself the questions that many were asking themselves at the time. My head was about to explode, who was I? Where was I going? What did I have to offer? I wanted to make a difference but I first needed something to make a difference in me. I was caught in between following Yahusha or carrying on as I had been. It's all about growing naturally but society doesn't give us that option. All that Yahusha did was love and bring positive vibes to the people. Everyone who followed what he said left his presence feeling better about life.

Hatred paralyzes life; love releases it.
Hatred confuses life; love harmonizes it.
Hatred darkens life; love illumines it.
Martin Luther King Jr

We are not here by chance or by accident. One sperm out of millions fertilised the egg that created you. What I mean is, we are not a mistake, we didn't come about by chance. We are not reactions but a response. We are a response of love. We are not just a part of this beautiful creation but its crowning glory. Creation has been abused and only now are we trying to treat it with the love and care we should have been. No, we are not just a part, but we are the best of it, the masterpiece. If you know anything about a masterpiece, it's not just thrown together but thought is put into it. Every detail is carefully thought through and is perfect in the creator's eye, only this qualifies it to be a masterpiece. This masterpiece, you and I are then born into a broken world, broken communities and, for some, a broken family. The reality is, when something is broken, stuff may leak through the cracks. Pain, hurt, abuse, hatred, judgement, bullying, fear, jealousy and all that stuff that poisons. We then measure our self-worth with the wrong unit of measurement. We are made by design and the biggest limiting belief is that we are lacking something. This broken world has taken away, it has damaged us, but we can be restored. He placed the music inside us that will reveal our purpose and how much YAHUAH loves us. Now the battle is on. We are the pride of creation, gifted to live a life of love and purpose. It's a trap we are not free to be, this broken world values the doers. They want our identity in what we do, not who we are. The foundation is not stable, we are more than that. We buy into the limiting theology as we limit ourselves and others. Inside, we have an aching, we know there's something more, we can faintly hear the music. We know we are not satisfied but we are afraid to share our heart's desire because if that is limited, we have nothing. We hide our dreams deep within and slog away day by day, losing ourselves in the process. But I say identity is the launch pad for destiny. We need to remember who we are. A masterpiece, the crown of creation. The things we are passionate about are a clue to our purpose, a clue to the music. That dream is inside us, so we can find our way, it's our internal Sat Nav towards our purpose and being. This broken world is always asking questions that limit us, but we are more. The world says you're ugly and offers you Botox or some other product. In truth, you are beautiful by design, created to bring joy. We are more than we have been conditioned to feel, we are those who bring value to others and our community. Even though it's broken, we don't need to buy into its brokenness but our being calling is to be who we are, ourselves. Bring value wherever you are. If this broken world has you twisted, don't give up or give in. It's in you, it's in all of us. Our creator left a little bit of him in each of us. This light must shine through our creative gifting. He gave us the gift of free will. We choose our attitude in every situation. There is a gap between stimulus and response. This is what makes our lives meaningful, it is this freedom that cannot be taken away. It is our responsibility to make things happen. Our behaviour is our own conscious choice based on values, rather than our environment, which is based on feelings. We empower what controls us. I am what I am by the choices I make. It's not what happens to us, but our response to what happens to us that hurts us. But today we understand who we are, and we are created to be dynamic, powerful, and beautiful. It's a choice, it's always a choice. I have a light inside, and I was made to shine!

I am YAHUAH's work of art, a masterpiece, a thing of beauty. I wanted my life to represent this truth. I had been contaminated; I had allowed what I had been through to live in me. It put me out of the flow that I needed to thrive in. YAHUAH knew me and touched me where I was in pain. My silent cry that expressed itself in anger and aggression was now replaced by a sense of peace. He knows the circumstances and situations we have experienced. He knows what we think about ourselves and it was up to me to take Him at His word! There is nothing more influential in shaping how we act than our self-image. If I see myself as weak and unable, I'll live it out. I never saw role models that looked like me apart from the ones that are vilified. I realised that black is beautiful and not something to be feared. A positive self-image will help me to develop the right sense of identity, I was able to find the balance. A journey that

211

started in hip hop was now complete. If I believe it, I can be it. It helped me understand who I was in relation to my old frustrations. It freed me from the bondage of other people's opinions. I can only be responsible for my actions and they speak louder than words. Our lives will be transformed if we grab hold of this truth. I was now positioned to fulfil my potential in life and be the man I was destined to be.

It is related of Michelangelo that, while walking with some friends through a street in Florence, he discovered a fine block of marble lying neglected and half buried in mud.

"There's an angel in the stone," he explained and straightway went to work clearing off the slime and mire, doing havoc to his holiday clothes. Taking the stone to his studio, he patiently toiled with mallet and chisel and finally let the angel out—in a statue of a beautiful angel.

When Michelangelo was asked what he was doing, he replied, "I'm liberating an angel from this stone." Sometimes we need to be liberated from the things that have held us, we need the areas chipped away so we can be free to express the fullness of who we are. Sometimes people only see the rock, we must see the angel. YAHUAH knows what we are and what kind of beauty is within us.

I started to let the rhymes flow and began to put pen to paper. I had no idea how it would come out; once again, I was breaking new ground. I had no idea how things would turn out, but I was ready for all possibilities. I knew it didn't mean anything now, but things were going to be okay. I was ready to face whatever came my way with a new-found strength. I wasn't looking for a genie to tend to my every wish, my need was to be loved and accepted for who I was. I was sick of being and feeling judged, now I felt the weight of a love that was willing to love me despite the many times I messed up. It was redemptive, and it was my redemption song.

> *"I'm mentally ready, the mics on I'm mentally steady.*
>
> *The bass line heavy my fingertips a little sweaty.*
>
> *I'm thinking about the things my father told me.*
>
> *Life it is a gift, take it slowly.*
>
> *I watched him closely, I watched my mother too.*
>
> *Who would have known years later, I'd be doing what they do?*
>
> *Searching for meaning, an answer to the questions that I got.*
>
> *I wanted fame, riches, ladies, I wanted the lot.*
>
> *Black consciousness it came in like a flood.*
>
> *Now you and I will be defined in relation to our blood.*
>
> *I wanted more I had a thirst, so I'd ignore.*
>
> *Every obstacle, opposition to the poor.*
>
> *I would sit and pray YAHUAH, are you real.*
>
> *So many layers how many of them are being peeled.*
>
> *Fragile roots, so I refuse the status quo.*
>
> *Open the box YAHUAH is bigger than you know".*

Yahusha died so I could live, and I wanted to live life to the fullest. Everything had changed for me now; I told Flaky, "I want to be real. I want to write and bring truth for all the heads that listen to hip hop. I want to let them know YAHUAH loves them without condition." It's not about what we can do, how articulate we are. It's not about how well we know the Bible or what gathering we go to. It's only about what YAHUAH has done, it opens the door for us all. The choice is yours! "That's the mission, to see as many know his love as possible." That's the way we began to think. I had stopped writing as I had become disillusioned with the scene. I felt the major labels were trying to control the culture through money. Now I had purpose, I was ready to explode at this point. I realised that the pain I had been through didn't need to live in me. I gave myself over to something and it was bigger than me. I was invited into the bigger story; I accepted the invitation. Everything about me, my passion, desires and dreams fitted perfectly within the bigger picture. I was part of a global canvas. It gave me focus and direction. If you aim at nothing, you hit it every time. I wanted

215

something real, something tangible, something I could relate to. I needed the change on the inside that would work its way to the outside. Yahusha Hamashiach made this real. He lived how I wanted to live, he maximised every encounter, every relationship, and he was real in every encounter. Everything He did was based on love. The type of love that would see a father give himself for his child. It is the type of love that moves beyond feelings and is encapsulated by actions. Sometimes you've got to do what you can and, only if necessary, use words. Some actions speak louder than words, it reminds me of the man that stood in front of the tank at Tiananmen Square, and how he found a cause worth dying for. I had found a cause worth living for. For too long, I had the attitude that I was ready to die; now I was ready to start living.

"I needed YAHUHA he didn't need a misfit like me.

I needed truth not religion for reality.

I sat in pews; I didn't want to sit anymore.

Disillusioned with the way we treat the poor.

The in betweeners, standing between me at what cost.

Control the masses all the while defying the cross.

I needed freedom and Yahusha came to set me free.

A morning service never really met my needs.

Relationship it describes the way I am with YAHUAH.

Now I'm hidden in the name of Yahusha.

More than a prayer a sinner has to pray or say.

It is a lifestyle that we should be living every day.

Don't want to feel guilty and have to hide my face.

Manipulated, when all I need is His grace.

Fragile roots, so I refuse the status quo.

Open the box YAHUAH is bigger than you know".

I needed to maximise my existence. It was time for me to live.

"Backslidden or walking in the Ruach of God.

Raising a family, it is a toast of all our love.

Walking and praying, I'm praying for real as I walk.

No need for talking for some the life they live is all talk.

Taking a verse regardless of the context.

> *Preaching a sermon so the people write cheques.*
>
> *Feeling so vex, and even on a bigger stage.*
>
> *Prepare the mood so the people feel amazed.*
>
> *Who's got the nicest building that's what they wanna know.*
>
> *Your church is growing a new building will help it grow.*
>
> *Let's raise a fund so pass the basket real slow.*
>
> *Buy your blessing as truth goes out the window.*
>
> *Fragile roots, so I refuse the status quo.*
>
> *Open the box YAHUAH is bigger than you know".*

Now I was starting on the front foot. Once I made the decision to follow Yahusha, I had a sense of peace that defied understanding. I was taking positive steps towards freedom, and as I did, the weight lifted and life came into perspective. Now I was ready to walk. I felt as light as air and as strong as I'd ever felt. The choice I made affected my life so dramatically, it was as dramatic as night and day, light and dark. I was now thirty-six years old and I loved Yahushua. It's about being free, a freedom worth living for. Today, I walk as a believer in Yahusha, living each day as best as I can. Not bound by religious organisation and denominations but in freedom. When you view life from the dancefloor, you see the immediate dancers around you. You are limited as you can't see beyond the heads around you. When you go upstairs and look over the balcony, you can see the whole dancefloor, the bigger picture, you can see how it all fits together. No longer was I a random puzzle piece, I found the global canvas I was born to be a part of. No matter what happens, we keep moving. What I believe will define my focus. No matter what my situation says, YAHUAH has good plans for my life as I seek the kingdom first. Our outcome is determined by our attitude and I can choose how I respond to life situations.

Yahusha lived a life of love no matter where he was,

Touching lives on the road leaving a legacy of love,

True love it is the essence of the one divine presence,

When you know the truth for real it is a blessing,

No need for second guessing, now you really see,

The mission we are on is to see another freed,

So that they can be, all that they can be,

That's why he birthed the ecclesia with the fire is key,

More than a building that is built bricks and mortar,

In the book of acts it was a people transformed by the father,

We need to return to the altar where we first saw his face,

When our motives were pure, do you remember that place.

In Saving Private Ryan, the squad had debated if it made sense for eight men to risk their lives to save one. There was no logic for it. They had hoped that Private Ryan's life was worth theirs. The final charge to Ryan was: 'Earn it,' that is, 'live your life in such a way so that our lives were worth dying for you'. Captain Miller repeats the charge again before he dies. I wake up each morning with the desire to maximise my abilities and YAHUAH-given talents.

Faith is to believe what you do not see; the reward of this faith is to see what you believe.

Saint Augustine

Reynolds

Chapter 10
Footprints in the concrete

Our deepest fear is not that we are inadequate. Our deepest fear is that we are powerful beyond measure. It is our light, not our darkness that most frightens us.' We ask ourselves, who am I to be brilliant, gorgeous, talented, fabulous? Actually, who are you not to be? You are a child of God. You're playing small does not serve the world. There's nothing enlightened about shrinking so that other people won't feel insecure around you. We are all meant to shine, as children do. We were born to make manifest the glory of God that is within us. It's not just in some of us; it's in everyone. And as we let our own light shine, we unconsciously give others permission to do the same. As we're liberated from our own fear, our presence automatically liberates others.

Marianne Williamson.

From the day I decided to become a follower of Yahusha, my desire to be a voice could never be quenched, the style and way to get it across did. I was working out what I was going through in rhymes.

> *"Sitting on a park bench wondering,*
>
> *How was I made, how was I created?*
>
> *Mmmmm I heard it was the 6th day,*
>
> *Yeah I heard it was the 6th day,*
>
> *Somebody told me I came from dust, could I trust?*
>
> *I knew to read the bible was a must,*
>
> *Naked I came forth and naked I will leave,*
>
> *My destiny hangs on whether I believe,*
>
> *Mmmmm let me think for a minute,*
>
> *The closer that I'm coming to the truth I'm feeling freer*
>
> *in my spirit,*
>
> *And I won't stop until I get there, It's so clear,*
>
> *I sense the truth is close for real I won't fear."*
>
> *I was full of life; you couldn't shut me up. I knew*

I was loved, I knew where I belonged, and I was a child of YAHUAH. I knew where I was going; I had a sense of destiny. I chose to appreciate the very thing that Yahusha offered up his life to give me: life. I decided to live life to the fullest I possibly could, making mature, responsible decisions based on the truth of Yahusha Hamashiach's life. I chose Yahusha because he first chose me, and I loved the way he loved and stood up to those who were fake. I loved how he put people before religion and loved outside the box. I like the way he painted word pictures to get his point across. Wherever he went, he exposed limiting beliefs and presented a limitless YAHUAH. Now I was relating to YAHUAH Elohim for real, through his Ruach Hakodesh. I was going to talk to him with words from my heart, now I pray with my eyes open.

"*Sweat drips, steady drip it's instrumental.*

Steady flip my potential, in the mental it's essential.

It resembles in my temple like an avatar.

My voice merges releasing an inner bar.

It transforms as I storm upon this platform.

I react to His spark now I'm getting warm.

Brings balance to the force just like Anakin.

Breaths life, life into this manikin.

It engages your heart like cerebro.

As I plug into his Ruach it detects flow.

Stimulates your mind to cause movement.

Your Impulses throb for improvement.

Your heart will never feel the same.

As I remain true to the game.

The time of His Ruach will never pass.

From the first to the last".

Times are rough and it seems we never have enough. It is in these times that we all need something to hold on to. I began to get involved in youth work and I was still trying to inspire the next generation. Young people on the edge of gangs, drugs, prison and death were my target to transmit life into. My goal was to spark something in them that might cause them to dream. This led me to write again; this led me to dream again. From the first to the last, I couldn't deny what I was: an emcee.

"From the first to the last, we be the new class.

New teacher to reach yer with the new pass.

Led by the presence of the Ruach that's within.

The seal of YAHUAH, when you're born again.

True freedom and I'm ready to select.

Respect to the soldiers with the Holy tech.

It drops next, from heartbeats to flat lines.

He leads me, now I see the signs.

You best believe, this walk is a tight squeeze.

I'm on a narrow road, ain't no room to slip please.

In a dark time, he is like a lantern.

Lighting up my way before He returns.

> *Bringing peace in the middle of the storm.*
>
> *Trend setters getting better and still getting warm.*
>
> *The time of His Ruach will never pass.*
>
> *From the first to the last".*

I think about rhyming all the time, *"Hard lines for me are hard rhymes, now more like a poet for these times."* Searching for truth should be an inspirational journey that leads to happiness, but there are so many whose own insecurities lead them to only feel secure if they are in control. I can only control my responses to life, not yours. Why should I frustrate myself in trying to make you behave the way I want? I always remember being told that actions are like a boomerang, they always come back. Sometimes the rule is broken and you can always look at cases to justify a certain point. But generally, if you're cool with others, they will be cool with you. So, be cool.

> *"From the first to the last.*
>
> *Yahweh remains true.*
>
> *His Spirit is the proof.*
>
> *His Spirit is the truth".*

Footprints are the impressions left behind by a person walking or running. Footprints can be followed as they leave a trail or tracks, so you can get to where the person you're following is.

One night I dreamed I was walking along the beach with the Lord.

Many scenes from my life flashed across the sky.

In each scene I noticed footprints in the sand. Sometimes there were two sets of footprints, other times there were one set of footprints.

This bothered me because I noticed that during the low periods of my life, when I was suffering from anguish, sorrow or defeat,

I could see only one set of footprints.

229

So I said to the Lord,

'You promised me Lord, that if I followed you, you would walk with me always.

But I have noticed that during the most trying periods of my life there have only been one set of footprints in the sand.

Why, when I needed you most, you have not been there for me?'

The Lord replied,

The times when you have seen only one set of footprints in the sand, is when I carried you.'

-Author Unknown

For many years, Beethoven couldn't hear a note of music, yet during this time, he composed some of his greatest masterpieces. At the opening performance of his Ninth Symphony, Beethoven conducted himself. He could not hear a single tone from the orchestra or chorus. At the close, the audience erupted into applause; Beethoven was oblivious of it until the lady who sang alto turned him around to face the audience. People were moved by the man who had to see instead of hearing the applause. He didn't let the fact that he was deaf destroy his passion. He held onto his dream. In the face of the assassin's bullet, growing hatred and opposition, Martin Luther King Jr dreamed of a better future. The Wright Brothers is a tale of failure, it is also the story of passion and flight.

So many people today are ready to die for something, an insult, a postcode, for being disrespected. Yet how many are ready to live for their dreams, their futures, and their destiny? Finding your music inside is like leaving footprints in the concrete, it is a privilege. Plant seeds of change that, once fully formed, could allow this generation to focus their energies in more productive places. Sacrifice is not a word we readily use anymore as we see overpaid individuals that lack the character and responsibility that comes with large amounts of money and influence. We need men and women to up their game, a generation who see themselves as a voice regardless of what society demands. Our lives will be successful as we navigate the obstacles that we are facing and will face. The world may write you off, but it's your job to always keep believing. You must push beyond the pain barrier and enter the part of the race where champions are made. No champ ever gained victory by quitting, so don't quit.

We are those who can shake the planet, it will impact my story and shape His story. Every dream, every pursuit of our YAHUAH-given potential means we are closer to be the men and women we were created to be. We must see the invisible in order for us to do the impossible. Before they were done, most things would have been considered impossible. Flight, a man on the moon. Someone saw it and dreamed it long before it was realised.

"We are like dwarfs sitting on the shoulders of giants. We see more, and things that are more distant, than they did, not because our sight is superior or because we are taller than they, but because they raise us up, and by their great stature add to ours."

John of Salisbury

We remember those that have gone before us for what they have done. We will be remembered for the things we have done. Leave your mark on the world and be remembered for something positive, something good – whether small or big. It is our time to make the best of what we can and do something good in the world. Our steps today are creating an impression for the future that influences others. Everyone leaves a footprint in concrete somewhere, though not everyone has the qualities or opportunity to leave such a footprint where it will be widely noticed. We need to be content with whatever impact our individuality brings to the ground we walk upon.

233

"Everyone has his own specific vocation or mission in life; everyone must carry out a concrete assignment that demands fulfillment. Therein he cannot be replaced, nor can his life be repeated. Thus, everyone's task is unique as is his specific opportunity to implement it."

Viktor E. Frank

We must ask ourselves, 'what does life expect from us?' Look into your future, there is always something that is expected from us. Be it as a father, brother, husband or friend, entrepreneur or creative, the questions are continually being asked. We must guard the hope in us that strengthens our ability to dream. If we are without hope, it leads to a decline resulting in a death of our dreams, our future, and last of all, our life purpose. We must not lose hope but remain courageous in whatever we are facing. To inspire courage, we look forward into the future. A future success, and from that point, we work back to our present. This will give us a map towards our dream. This will help bridge the gap between what you are to what you can become. Everyone has his own specific calling, their mission in life that demands fulfilment. Every situation they face, they do so in the knowledge of their mission in life, and through this, they find the strength to overcome the obstacles they face. I don't question life, but life is continually questioning me. It is my life purpose to inspire as that helps me define my answer to what it throws up. I followed the footprints and they led me to a love so real and dynamic it has redefined me. I am what I am through the choices I have made. When we think about the talents of the next generation, we can learn a lesson from hip hop. A group of people got together and made something out of nothing, and that nothing has come to define an entire era. In language, fashion, attitudes, and art, that nothing, that thing that was invisible was that dream, that passion. Once it has been seen and acted upon, it is able to make the invisible manifest. It will transform our future. My faith has the power to do so much more!

When I say that daddies near.

There's only a few filled with fear as the masses don't care.

The wickedness is very clear.

Sweet dreams of YAHUAH or our own nightmare.

Laws of love I compare.

With society today greed and hate so many share.

For the end we must prepare.

See the signs in the times make your move if you dare.

El Shaddai Elohim.

Ain't no secrets in the game if you want to be redeemed.

YAHUSHA my Lord.

We spread the news of the King like we're going on tour.

While you're screaming out for peace.

Outside of YAHUAH watch the madness increase.

In the belly of the beast.

> *The wicked feast on each other and we know it won't*
>
> *cease.*

Every great dream begins with a dreamer. Always remember, you have within you the strength, the patience, and the passion to reach for the stars to change the world.

Harriet Tubman

I have said this already, 'It takes a village to raise a child.' But our villages are fractured by mistrust and fear. Our most vulnerable in our communities will always suffer. It was for those I wanted to be a voice, to make a difference. Many lacked the opportunity and level of aspiration to reach above the stereotypes, prejudice and stigma. It was these very same obstacles I had to rise above to live my dream. Society condemns them for dreaming and pushes them towards the mundane. Their dreams and aspirations have been attacked and we are living their reaction. We don't value their potential and we are a poorer society as a result. Hip hop was a reaction to poverty, to lack, to being overlooked and ignored.

We must stop looking at others and thinking, 'what do they have to offer?' Turn it around. How can we help them fulfil their huge potential? Teachers must not categorize young people by culture or behaviour. Behaviour is a simplistic response to a complicated stimulus. Just because one has a better environment should not mean they are treated better than one who has not. A system built on privilege can only result in anarchy. We must help our world heal. We must look after our environment, look after nature. Yet first things first, we must look after each generation, giving them the love and support that can be the launch pad for their success. We must look beyond the hard exterior, the clothes, the walk, the talk. We must look beyond the behaviour, the mistakes and help solidify their foundation. No structure built on a weak foundation will last – it's an accident waiting to happen. Businesses must invest in this generation; opportunities must be spread out before them. Many have made choices to join groups because society has failed them. We cannot keep acting the same way and expect different results. It is time to change. As a people, what are we becoming? Change is fundamentally a human characteristic. A baby is born with the potential inside to be a man or woman. Throughout their lives, they are becoming as they transition through life. For those that have made bad choices, there is still hope. They can still become something they aspired to be as a child. Sometimes we need to awaken the inner dream and go back to when life made sense and reroute the GPS. We may need to rewire the neural pathways of our minds. Everyone who has experienced success realises that, to achieve what they did, they had to sit on the shoulders of giants. I don't understand the reluctance to allow others to sit on ours. We all have a part to play within the villages we journey through. Let's all leave footprints others can follow.

Don't stop dreaming!

Chapter 11
Echoes

The best of a book is not the thought which it contains, but the thought which it suggests; just as the charm of music dwells not in the tones but in the echoes of our hearts.

John Greenleaf Whittier

We all have a deep-rooted need to belong, it was this feeling that led me in search of a movement. Somewhere to belong or something to belong to. That sense of belonging can drive us into the arms of many, some who might not have our best interests at heart and others that do. It is so important to know the difference. I felt a deep disconnect within society, what I looked like seemed to matter more than what was in my heart. I was always looking for people that would echo what was in my heart and send it back. I was drawn to them.

First a feeling to a thought, thought to a rhyme,

Rhymes base for the rhythm to align,

Converge as the sounds combine,

From your ear to your spine,

The echoes going around,

Listen to the sound, listen to the sound,

Rebounds coming back around,

Mainstream and underground,

In tune so we are immune,

Free world yeah we're coming soon,

Uplift yes we bring hope,

Move quick so you can cope,

Don't slip, I go for broke,

We shift or you will choke,

Big rift, in the mazes of life,

Blinded in the hazes of strife,

Complex thoughts like a vet,

Detect as necks get wrecked,

With tech all the souls from old,

Respect the brave and the bold,

> *Stay pure so raw from the hate,*
>
> *No law by the door of your fate,*
>
> *The floor shake no break in the tempo,*
>
> *All around me echoes.*

I was visiting Kensington Temple. A friend of mine whose family performed together were in concert. It was a Friday night and I wanted to have fun. When I arrived, the service had already begun. It was packed and I thought that I would have to stand. I recognised one of the ushers, his wife was a close friend of my mother. He led me to the balcony where there were two seats available. I couldn't wait for the Noel's to hit the stage. As a band, they were so tight, and Susie and Hazel sang like old school soul divas. The music was pumped up and the whole place was rocking. A short time later, the same usher returned – unbeknown to me, I was having too much of a good time. I didn't notice the fine young lady who sat next to me. It was the only seat left in the building. I was rocking my two-step trying not to step on the toes of those next to me. The whole place was in unity, it is the power of music. The atmosphere was positive and full of energy. This kind of atmosphere reminded me of shows I had been involved in, it made me feel alive. Before you knew it, Kenton Noel was introducing his brothers, James and Phillip, and his sisters, Susie and Hazel. That was a good night. As I sat down, I turned to the lady on my right and began to share how tight that was. We began talking like we had known each other for years. We made our way down to the café and continued talking, I was oblivious to anything or anyone else. As she was about to leave, I did the gentlemanly thing by walking her to Notting Hill Gate station. She gave me her house number; I didn't have a phone where I was staying. I did it the old-school way, going to the phone box to make calls. Our friendship grew and developed over the next few months and years.

Nothing is impossible, the word itself says "I'm possible"!
Audrey Hepburn

The wrong relationship can break you. It can grind you down, one brick at a time. Who you choose to spend the rest of your life with cannot be based on just an emotional feeling. My life choice had to be a little deeper than that. I was taught many things in school that I have never used again and many things that I should have learned were never taught. I wasn't taught how to manage and use money to make money. I wasn't taught about love and what it is. Hollywood and the latest songs gave us their insight. Luckily for me, I had two parents that modelled marriage for me. Not everyone has that and so you can end up looking for what is familiar to you, regardless of how destructive it may be. My wife has been a cheerleader for me when I haven't believed in myself. Every successful person in life will point to someone who was their biggest cheerleader, who believed in them when it was just a dream. I was going to propose to mine.

> You see my minds on point,
>
> Digging deep to anoint every joint,
>
> Every word to a verb you heard,
>
> Every word never slurred transferred,
>
> It's a God given gift,
>
> Drops, rhyme, echoes, lifts,
>
> I take a thought using words as my ink,
>
> Reaching minds on the brink,
>
> I place a link in this,
>
> Don't blink, you can't resist,
>
> I'm getting into this,
>
> Just think, you must persist,
>
> Play list to the sound you hear,
>
> Every year show no fear,
>
> No tears so let me get lyrical,
>
> You can call it a miracle,
>
> See I'm like a Titan,
>
> On the shoulder of giants,

> *Hearing echoes like the roar of a Lion,*
>
> *To the past I'm so reliant,*
>
> *True warriors, so defiant,*
>
> *Hear the echoes from life's true giants,*
>
> *Rebound, you can't see the sign in,*
>
> *To the ground perfect timing,*

I was still connected to the music industry, working with Ronnie Wilson and Dennis Charles. I was the rap coach, I worked in conjunction with them on Eternal's debut album, M'n'8 and Michelle Gayle. It kept feeding my inner performer and the music inside. My journey of self-discovery, for a short while, remained motionless while I performed. I felt now I was heading towards something new. I had no idea what it would be. I did not feel as vulnerable as I thought, as this time, I had someone by my side. On the 30th of September 1995, I was married in Leyton Elim Church. Me one became me two and now I was starting a family of my own. It was a memorable day, as it was a time of celebration and reflection with my wider family. My life soon became my family and I lost focus and ignored the music inside. I thought I was doing the right thing by becoming responsible. It was always drummed into me that I am the provider, that is who I am. I let go of that entrepreneurial spirit that I had attained during my days as a hip hop pioneer. I started to follow the status quo. Work, eat, sleep, repeat was the new mantra of my life and it was killing me. In 1999, I had one of the most life-impacting events I will ever have. I witnessed the birth of my son, Tre. We called him Tre as he would have been our third child as we had experienced two miscarriages. A year before he was born, my father passed on and my foundation felt unstable. Life seemed to be on autopilot. In 2002, my beautiful daughter, Renee, was born; she was a ray of sunshine. My life continued; eat, sleep and repeat. We visited some beautiful countries following the blueprint we have been exposed to. The thing was, this blueprint wasn't my music.

I have learned over the years that when one's mind is made up, this diminishes fear.

Rosa Parks

In 2005, I moved to Liverpool, away from family and friends. We started a men's recovery home in our house. We would take men who had been controlled by substances and support them in kicking the habit. We reached out to prostitutes to see how we could best support them. I met some beautiful people whose circumstances had been against them. From a 16-year-old girl kept in a flat by a middle-aged man. He supplied her with drugs for sex. I managed to see her return to her family from the north east of England. Stacy was a tipping point for me, she had been selling her body for drugs since she was twelve. Let that sink in, she had slipped through the net and was now being abused for pocket change. At times, I would give her the money she needed so she didn't have to sleep with anyone, but I knew it was really helping her. She stayed one night with my family and spent the whole night cuddling one of my daughter's soft toys. We had arranged for another lady to go into rehab, but she was murdered the night before. It was during this time in 2006 that my son, Jaeden, was born.

A truly rich man is one whose children run into his arms when his hands are empty.

Author Unknown

What's money? A man is a success if he gets up in the morning and goes to bed at night and in between does what he wants to do.

Bob Dylan

We stopped the work in 2009 as it was taking a high emotional toll. I wasn't happy, my music inside was dormant. I enjoyed making a difference in people's lives, but my music is not like that. In 2010, my youngest son was born, Theodore Cruz. I had a great family and I was doing the normal routine. In a job that I didn't find satisfying but it paid the bills. I worked in children's homes, youth centres, youth information shops, referral units and schools and would return home frustrated and angry. It felt that these institutions were not built to help young people fly. No, it seemed it was about creating sheep, yes men and woman. Ones who would wear what they are told and do what they are told. The music inside didn't matter as dreams won't pay the bills. Tell that to Richard Branson!

Was I ready to live the life that I felt I deserved? As a child, you live carefree and all who see you celebrated your cuteness. They encouraged you to sing, to act, to be a lawyer, teacher, astronaut or prime minister, they encouraged our creative energy. When you become an adult, caution precedes celebration. 'You can't' replaces 'yes you can' as encouragement is replaced by restraint. We learn to hide in plain sight as we bury our dreams deep within us. We shudder at the thought of showing who we are, we feel the need to protect our inner child. We develop the mindset that if we stand out, we will get shot down. So, we blend in and become like everyone else – a human chameleon. Living a totally normal existence when there's nothing normal about us. I would get so frustrated as my music was being suppressed. My job was killing my creativity.

My emotional outbursts were out of context to the situation I was facing. Again and again, I would feel backed into a corner and blow. I needed to stop denying who I was and make the decisions that would release my potential. You can deny your values all you want, but sooner rather than later, it will be leaking through your behaviour. I was sick of leaking, I started to contemplate rapping again. Inspiring people is important to me along with performing. I am a showman at heart who wants to deliver a powerful message. Being on stage made me feel fulfilled. I would wake up in the morning excited and on the front foot. As I played my music inside, the real me introduced himself to the world. The more I played my music, the stronger I became. The more I was able to deal with the negativity and negative people.

> *From the back to the front, front to the back,*
>
> *It's our own book of acts,*
>
> *Many see but so many can't,*
>
> *Who'll speak for those that aren't,*
>
> *Who listens to the righteous chant?*
>
> *Pure seeds, that are too hard to plant?*
>
> *I see so many giving in,*
>
> *It's the times that we're living in,*
>
> *No vision, stops you from moving,*
>
> *No direction, our minds need retuning,*

> *All systems go, my energy it's consuming*
>
> *I won't quit, see I know what I'm doing,*
>
> *We aspire from the mire not losing,*
>
> *Using the truth as my proof as I'm cruising,*
>
> *Before I step in, it's a win win,*
>
> *I hear the echoes from the past now I begin.*

I was talking to my sister, Janet, who had completed a Life Coaching course. Again and again, she was pushing me towards it. She took the bold step of enrolling me on an online coaching course. A mind in motion will remain in motion unless it's disturbed by an outside force. It awakened something inside, it stirred my music. My inner performer began to rise to the surface. I wanted to return to the stage, to inspire, to help others find their music. I found my music early in life and then allowed the pressures of life to crush it. But that's not the end, that dream was inside me. When I connected to my passion of speaking and performing, I heard my music. I remembered my music and what it felt like to play it. I realised my unique message; I deliver a coaching message in an inspirational way to help people find their music inside. It was still on the stage; it was still performing, and it was still using words.

Look how far we have fallen from, so many wrong in a song,

Just a reminder of where we belong,

We bring on to your conscious, as we awaken,

No shorts taken weak minds get shaken,

Vacant minds has fake thugs gripping the mic,

Lacking the bite, they all are loving the hype,

Real talk for the real talk forgets the merk talk,

Alter egos on the mic that you can't walk,

We used to want to uplift the mind,

Now we struggle in the clutch with no truth to find,

Insecure and what's more you must be lacking in size,

Grab your crutch, release the clutch, the return of the wise,

From a rapper to a gangster smooth like Casanova,

> No, we won't roll over, need the truth of YAHUAH,
>
> Rappers spit rhymes that are mostly illegal,
>
> Hip hop is a way to uplift our people.

Some people live their life according to the rule that believing is seeing. Within our imagination, we see our dreams before they have materialised. We see the invisible that is within the realm of our hearts and we bring it into physical existence by actioning our goals. Sometimes all we have is a word that resonates inside us, it sparks a passion response. Without faith in ourselves, we will never take the necessary steps we need to take. That is why you can't surround yourself with negative people. Negativity eats away at our faith; faith in ourselves and faith in our skills. It could stop our forward momentum so we are not as effective as we could be. Our battle is to keep on believing and not to settle for what others say but settle for what you have seen. I visualize my outcomes and then work towards them.

Freefall in a minute, so grab the ledge,

When you're in it, you got to win it or you'll be dead,

On the crest of a wave you're like a slave in a system

that says,

You're going to fail like from back in the days,

We change our ways in the cypher as we structure the

plan,

So, we can reach you fam, we got the outstretched hand,

The majority's poverty no authority economy's

ferocity's mockery, as it hits the minority,

With velocity they strike at the blink of an eye,

While my people in the ends are happy chasing the lie,

They tried to fool us to think a thug life gave way,

What we see today is just the mind of the slave,

Still in the trade we make a raid for your freedom of

thought,

Bringing you the truth from the kingdom where no

souls are bought,

In the times that we're living in hear me people,

We're in freefall.

All faith gets tested, we can all hit obstacles and setbacks. Our response must always be to get back up. When I taught my son to ride his bike, I put him on the bike and gave him a push. I shouted, 'keep peddling and you won't fall'. The first time he fell, what did he do? He got back up and started peddling again. If we hit a wall, why can't you just get back on the bike?

Falling can't you hear us calling,

So many young minds are forgotten by the morning,

Fake thugs warring, rich pimps is boring,

Young ones are whoring while where free falling,

Trying to make a way in this game it's my calling,

Gun shots blast to the yes yalling

What goes up comes down heed the warning,

Lifestyles of the rich cause we're balling, as were free

falling,

Every opportunity before you is a doorway to greater experiences. That is why we learn from every failure, not to give up but to get it right. When you believe something is going to happen, you prepare for it, you live for it. Success does not happen by chance but by purposeful acts towards a desired goal.

I would rather die of passion than of boredom.
Vincent van Gogh

A person who never made a mistake never tried anything new.
Albert Einstein

I have a heart for young people, to see them released towards their potential. To see them dream bigger dreams and realise their music. To see their aspirations magnified, and for some, implanted into their consciousness. To see them live the life they could only dream of. I look at my children and I want to give them a launch pad. I want them to dream, I want you to dream. Not just dream but to dream big. Impossible is nothing.

"Cemeteries are full of unfulfilled dreams... countless echoes of 'could have' and 'should have'... countless books unwritten... countless songs unsung... I want to live my life in such a way that when my body is laid to rest, it will be a well needed rest from a life well lived, a song well sung, a book well written, opportunities well explored, and a love well expressed."

Steve Maraboli

Chapter 12
Inspire the Fire

"Set your life on fire. Seek those who fan your flames"
Rumi

What would your world be like if you did the things that created more meaning to your life? Purpose, meaning and fulfilment are not ideals beyond our reach. They are the very things that are within us. It is the music inside that defines who we are. We all have talents and gifts, and the world is a richer place when we become who we are made to be. We are taught to be safe and chase normality. Limiting beliefs bombard you as you dare to dream. It starts with a dream; it always starts with a dream. We see the invisible first before it is realised, thought produces the action. Many situations can arise that can kill our dreams and infect our hearts. This causes us to live below our designated life purpose. For this reason, many deny the music inside and deny true freedom and happiness. Imagine if that spark is reignited. Imagine that passion not just catching alight, imagine it ablaze. To blaze means to make a mark, usually indicating a path – he blazed his way through the storm. I am using the term blaze to describe a life on fire, full of purpose and direction. We want to live a life blazing a path that encourages others to do the same. John Wesley said, *"I set myself on fire and people come out to watch me burn"*. To see us reaching and influencing the lives of our peers, reassuring them they have a unique identity, a place where they can belong. Helping them in visualising a positive future, giving them something to aim for. How good would it be to see us set free of the limitations that are placed on us, and use this platform so we can connect with our purpose and maximize our potential and creativity with confidence? To see a generation living without the masks and live without the false expectations placed on them.

"It takes your knowing to decide on your going. If you know where you are going, you will keep going because you have already seen yourself gone"

Israelmore Ayivor

Being ablaze is continuing to push forward, to strive to reach a goal or objective despite the many discouragements, setbacks or loss of faith. It is keeping faith with your mission, purpose, or set of values long after the others have thrown in the towel, that is the pathway to success. The world is full of people who are more than willing to tell you all the reasons why you can't follow your dream or succeed at something others haven't done yet. Vision is about creating something new, built upon the foundation of the past and the present, emerging with a reality that is better than that which is currently available. When fully enacted, vision brings us closer to our ideals. We must be the ones who do things on purpose. Wake up focused and be purpose-driven. We won't be successful by mistake, but by a well thought out strategy of faith and love. We must love on purpose, give of ourselves on purpose, reach out on purpose until being on purpose is our natural response. That is when we will see the blaze.

Can I get your attention?

The rhyme drops can you feel the connection,

It's like a wave and it's moving in sections,

Front to back this is the direction,

I keep moving the key is will you follow me,

If you're propping up the walls then it bothers me,

If you're looking for a squabble then unfollow me,

If hate is in your heart listen to me,

Get in the flow, coz real life is in this,

It's like a light, and so I'm moving with this,

I'm dreaming good times, like it's supposed to be,

It's Reynolds why don't you come with me.

Within hip hop culture, much of the artist's success depends on how they "represent". To represent in a hip hop context in large part means to be true to one's self. For other hip hop artists, the success of their careers has not been based on keeping it real, but instead on wearing a mask or adopting an alter ego. Life can play out in different ways. You may end up having many different identities and wearing various masks for various reasons. You can wear them for so long that you forget who you are. Peer pressure is a powerful force that squeezes our identity. We must resist its subtle advances and be advocators of individuality. One of the major truths of the gospel that spoke to me was the fact that I was made by design.

For we are YAHUAH's making, created in union with the

Yahusha Hammishiach for a life of good actions already

prepared by YAHUAH for us to do.

Ephesians 2:10

We follow the footprints of others, not to become clones but to learn from their journey. We celebrate their victories and allow the realisation of their success to penetrate our beings. If they can do it, so can I, if I work hard and choose life at those moments when we are questioned by our circumstances.

We Wear the Mask by Paul Laurence Dunbar

We wear the mask that grins and lies,

It hides our cheeks and shades our eyes,

This debt we pay to human guile;

With torn and bleeding hearts we smile,

And mouth with myriad subtleties.

Why should the world be otherwise,

In counting all our tears and sighs?

Nay, let them only see us, while

We wear the mask.

We smile, but, O great Christ, our cries

To thee from tortured souls arise.

We sing, but oh the clay is vile

> *Beneath our feet, and long the mile;*
>
> *But let the world dream otherwise,*
>
> *We wear the mask!*

Sometimes we struggle against incredible obstacles. It can feel like they are impossible to overcome. At times, it seems easier to wear a mask to shield your heart from rejection. This keeps us from sharing our dreams and passions. I believe whatever dream we may have, we also have the strength to break through the barrier.

> *When I see you living life it's a hype thing?*
>
> *Each step I take and we in full swing,*
>
> *Dance in the moment, I just love the bass lick,*
>
> *Inspire fire as the melody and drum kick,*
>
> *See I love the way the Ruach's moving it,*
>
> *Feel the rhythm in your spine while you're living it,*
>
> *All the troubles of the day you are losing it,*
>
> *Your heart ached in the past so where soothing it,*

> *Negative words are depressing so where moving it,*
>
> *Raise your eyes to the dream where pursuing it,*
>
> *All your friends along the way, not forgetting them,*
>
> *I know myself who I am so I'm bringing them,*
>
> *We be doing this until the early morning,*
>
> *We ain't stopping until all hearts are burning,*
>
> *And now you're calling me, the host of heaven are*
>
> *supporting me,*
>
> *Fan the flame in your heart, why don't you come with*
>
> *me.*

Finding the music is all about motivating us to realise our dreams and help provide the focus to make them come true. Despite the hardships and conflicts that we face on the way to our dreams, we realise our life purpose is worth pursuing. Sometimes we must go against the odds, against the opinion of others and learn to swim against the flow. By focusing and realising our dreams, we learn to survive despite the negativity that pulls us back.

The Rose That Grew from Concrete

Did you hear about the rose that grew from a crack in the

concrete?

Proving nature's law is wrong it learned to walk without

having feet.

Funny it seems, but by keeping its dreams, it learned to

breathe fresh air.

Long live the rose that grew from concrete when no one

else ever cared.

By **Tupac Shakur**

Sometimes we must struggle against incredible obstacles. It can feel like they are impossible to overcome. Amazingly, we often end up finding that we have the strength to break through the barrier. The Rose that Grew from the Concrete is about reaching our goals in life despite the hardships and conflicts that we face on the way. The poem is highly inspirational as was its writer, Tupac Shakur. Has anyone ever told you that you could not do something? That you are incapable of accomplishing a goal you set out to complete? How did you feel? What did you do?

The rose defied nature to grow, sometimes you must see the invisible to do the impossible. The rose has learnt how to walk without having feet. By focusing and realizing its dreams, it finally learnt to survive within an environment that other roses would have died in. Its harsh surrounding did not prove to be a hindrance to the rose's growth. You may feel incomplete, unsettled and unfulfilled, with a driving need to fill the holes in your lives. This need may produce feelings of insecurity and you may desire to fill that hole with whatever will put an end to the pain. Some try to silence the pain with whatever they can; alcohol or drugs, sex or a pattern of controlled behaviour. We need to remove the obstacles that hinder us from knowing who we really are. We need to bring the shady areas in our lives into the light.

We have heard the saying 'the early bird gets the worm'. This is true but so do all the other birds get a worm. There are more than enough worms to go around. In the same way there is a place for each of us to fulfil our dreams and be complimentary of each other as we come together in the greater story. It is within the greater story that our purpose and passion are realised. It is our responsibility to make something happen. It is in that place we understand that our behaviour is a function of our decisions, not our conditions. I am what choices I have made.

> *We hit the floor so hard we're like titans,*
>
> *We go hard you would think we were violent,*
>
> *To see our dreams fulfilled we can't be silent,*
>
> *I need more strength in my cup,*
>
> *On the road of life, it's not down to luck,*
>
> *To the right move and just sway a bit,*
>
> *You can do it, I know that you're feeling it,*
>
> *To know your purpose in life, there's no need to fear,*
>
> *Inside your passion are the keys to why you're here,*
>
> *No stress, we dress so we can impress,*

> *I confess my dream, reveals I will bless,*
>
> *In every test, I follow the light he gives me,*
>
> *No regrets, I'm living the life I dreamed see.*
>
> *As we move the pressure heightens,*

People can have enough to live by but nothing to live for; they have the means but no meaning. There is always a solution to the problem, an answer to life's questions or meaning to life. You must stay in the game to win it; only then will you see the answer of what you so diligently seek.

The well-known village atheist was seen running vigorously to the site of a burning church building, intent on joining with others in helping to extinguish the flames. A neighbour, observing him, exclaimed in amazement, "This is something new for you! I never saw you going to church before!" The atheist replied, "Well, this is the first time I've ever seen a church on FIRE before!"

Author Unknown

The fire must never go out, it must be kept burning, it must give off its light. When Yahusha walked, he was the light. Through our gifts and passion, we reflect that light. Eric Liddell said, "God made me fast. And when I run I feel his pleasure." He found his music and ran with it. Those dreams that are inside us are clues to our divine purpose. The moon has a glow that can light the night, but the source of its light is a reflection of the sun.

A man returning from a journey brought his wife a matchbox that would glow in the dark. After giving it to her she turned out the light, but the matchbox could not be seen. Both thought they had been cheated. Then the wife noticed some French words on the box and asked a friend to translate them. The inscription said: "If you want me to shine in the night, keep me in the light."

Who am I? I am a creative, and as I walk in who I was designed to be, I will stand out as unique and powerful. As we all are unique and powerful. We have the unique ability to bring something out of nothing, to reach within and take a thought, a dream and see it transform into a reality. This gift, this ability brings us closer to YAHUAH than many realise. It connects us with our music inside. It could be a song, a rap, a piece of art, a dance, a story, an idea, as we draw out what is within us. My creative identity gives me the foundation to overcome the many limiting beliefs that exist. As I overcome them, my light will shine brighter. My passion and purpose drives me towards this end, to see these limiting beliefs broken in the minds of every person I'm in contact with. I am a light and I was designed to shine. To share my light so others can shine. To see as many lights shine together so we can blaze.

Today I choose life. Every morning when I wake up I can choose joy, happiness, negativity, pain... To feel the freedom that comes from being able to continue to make mistakes and choices - today I choose to feel life, not to deny my humanity but embrace it.

Kevyn Aucoin

"We are not human beings on a spiritual journey. We are spiritual beings on a human journey".

Stephen Covey

Always remember the main things that limit us are the size of our vision and our own self-limiting beliefs. You are what you think you are. We must learn to recognise our human tendencies; they help us understand why we do what we do. We will then be able to consciously choose our responses rather than reacting. It is time to set goals and develop a strategy so you can do what you love, what is my purpose? Always start with the end in mind and work towards it. Be the best version of yourself, fight against limiting beliefs wherever you stumble upon them. Let our lights shine until we blaze and become that beacon that warns others on this journey where the rocks and pitfalls are. The lighthouse reminds us that, regardless of how turbulent the seas may become, we need only to steer towards the light. So, blaze wherever you are, be that light wherever darkness presents itself. Never forget who we have inside us, creation itself is thirsty for the revealing of the sons and daughters of YAHUAH. When the sons and daughters of YAHUAH are revealed, when the presence and Kingdom of YAHUAH is manifested in us and through us, when we meet with Yahusha, something happens in the natural world. When we connect with His Ruach in us, when we bring forth his Kingdom into our present reality, something happens between heaven and earth when we, as the children of YAHUAH, encounter YAHUAH and His powerful presence.

Chapter 13

The pictures you see are the pictures you will be!

Life is full of beauty. Notice it. Notice the bumble bee, the small child, and the smiling faces. Smell the rain and feel the wind. Live your life to the fullest potential, and fight for your dreams.

Ashley Smith

Keep away from people who try to belittle your ambitions. Small people always do that, but the really great make you feel that you, too, can become great.

Mark Twain

I heard someone say you can only be it if you see it. People will encourage you by saying 'make that dream a reality'. Believing is seeing. At times, it is the only way we can be all that we have been made to be. Sometimes all you have is a dream, formed in the quiet place of your heart. It hasn't been spoken about, but you see it whenever you have the space to imagine. We believe for something that, when you look at the facts, you have no evidence in the natural world to back up your belief. You're not skilled in that area, you don't have the experience or training. All you have is your dream. *First, you must see the invisible before you can do the impossible!*

When I look back at my humble beginnings, I was in my bedroom in front of my mirror. I was rapping over instrumental records to an audience of one. I didn't realise my competency level as I thought I was great. I became conscious of my competency the first time I rapped in front of an audience. Sometimes we need to step out and act on our dream. Every negative response and critical word attacks our dream and can weaken our resolve. Believing you can will keep you pushing so you can maintain forward momentum. Negative words attack our confidence, so we don't step out and be as effective as we could be. Our battle is to keep on believing and not to settle for what we see. At times, people tell you what they see, but if it's not as great as I see, then I must ignore what may be limiting. The biggest negative voice that limits us can be ourselves. 'I can't', 'it won't work', 'I'm not that good'. It is within this testing that our dreams can be refined, if we stay in the process. An old-fashioned Blacksmith would heat the metal until it was so hot that the dross and impurities would burn away. Sometimes it gets so hot that we give up, we let go. I had to keep going, I became a student of the art. I worked on my delivery, stage presence and performance. I practised my dance moves so I could give an all-round performance. So many things had the title 'never been done', but someone stayed in the process, rode the waves of negativity until their dream became a reality. It's not enough if all you do is dream; you must act upon it. Success is not a chance happening, but small actions made on purpose. Adjustments to my attitude and lifestyle and positioning myself for success. I practised and practised until I developed the right kind of habits. Now I could perform without thinking, it was etched into my patterns of behaviour.

First, I had to see my dream, imagine what it looks like. Seeing myself on stage with the crowd going wild. When you can see it, work backwards and set goals to fulfil it. Goal setting must be targeted and strategic. I had to see the end and work backwards. It must lead towards the dream and its fulfilment. It's time to get busy! Busy people haven't got time for negativity or negative people. If they aren't rowing in your direction, they need to get out of the boat. You need to focus on the things that reinforce your creative gifting. What is at stake for you? Don't allow anything to mess with it. Every opportunity before you is the doorway to a greater experience.

Verbalising your dream can have a similar effect to seeing it. It can help you to step away from the issue that had you broken and step into the process that can shape you. Failure is often the stepping stone to success, as long as you don't give up. As soon as you decide to believe, then your dream can be realised. I remember being told that you couldn't make a living as a rapper. Yet my dream was so entwined in who I was, it was a battle not to take things personally. At times, we must confront our self-image. I don't look or sound like what is popular. Is there a gap in the market for what I do? I had to resist giving up my identity to be like the hype rapper at the time. If I had copied, I could only go as far as the person I was copying. In the midst of it all, the unpredictability, all you can do is keep on keeping on. In the face of discouragement, all you can do is keep on singing, writing, being the creative soul you are destined to be. In the face of criticism and being misunderstood, remember your dream and how it makes you feel. When people tell you to get real, tell them you're being as real as real can be. If you're worried about your self-image, you don't want to look crazy, you must understand you do not want to miss out on your dream because of someone else's unreal expectations. We all have a set of beliefs that define us, who we are and what we can or will not do. Our beliefs about ourselves are the strongest force shaping our lives. Our belief will dictate our behaviour.

If I don't see it, I won't be it. I see myself engaging the hearts and minds of those I can reach. As I look back, these have been informative years. Learning, reading and enlarging my capacity so I can fulfil my potential and embody my dream. An old-school mentality having to adjust to a new school scene, we call this flipping the script. You don't have to stay where you are, your outer world will always reflect your inner world. Work on your character, educate yourself, prepare for success. It doesn't happen by chance; it is something that is done on purpose. Goals are intentional so you can realise your dream. Plans are made so you stay on course. Responsibility is taken as you have the power to choose. If things are not happening, look in the mirror and make the necessary changes that will allow for growth and success. Who said you can't teach an old dog new tricks? That type of negativity needs to be binned.

Two roads diverged in a wood and I - I took the one less traveled by, and that has made all the difference.

Robert Frost

The relationship between storytelling in the village and making a difference within a generation are similar paths. The goal is to see more potential released on the world. I often imagine all that positive energy and what it would mean to our tribes that we identify with. I used my lyrics to inspire the listeners exposing them to an alternate view. I know that if we all came together, it represents a much more powerful entity than being separate. That was the beauty behind the B.R.O.T.H.E.R. Movement. Whatever your background, we all have common goals, so we smash the barriers placed in between us so we can achieve our potential and continue to advance as the people we were created to be. I dreamed of using my voice to challenge the status quo, through current events and personal narratives. I wanted my audience to enjoy my words, but I also wanted it to make a difference in their lives. It was all about creating awareness and imparting knowledge. I was driven by the principle that social change came through knowledge of self and personal discovery. I wanted to reflect and transmit the truth that we can be what we dream.

> *"Well I'm a brother whose sliding reason I defy,*
>
> *I can't hide from the truth, I won't lie,*
>
> *Lies are like sinking sand,*
>
> *For me to make it through I gotta watch how I stand,*
>
> *The way I act they saw me as a problem child,*
>
> *I learned your ways but I have my own style,*
>
> *So, I figure, be the father figure,*

> *Coming up you know it's sicker, kids are quicker with the trigger,*
>
> *So many struggles that's why they hit the liquor,*
>
> *A silent killer, you're own thriller in Manila,*
>
> *It's so bitter, there's so many pages,*
>
> *So many rages, packed in concrete cages,*
>
> *How many say that they do it for the endz,*
>
> *Killed for the postcode we're losing all our mens,*
>
> *Your destination is set from the choices you made,*
>
> *Now who's getting played?"*

People may tell you that you have lots of potential, but they will say you are wasting it. Some young people have been told that they have none. Yet do we really understand what potential is? Do we understand that by discovering our potential it will literally redefine our destiny? Knowing your potential changes your life by helping you understand what you can thrive at and who you can become. Knowing that allows you to overcome your present situation and be your dream.

I am here for a purpose and that purpose is to grow into a mountain, not to shrink to a grain of sand. Henceforth will I apply ALL my efforts to become the highest mountain of all and I will strain my potential until it cries for mercy.

Og Mandino

We all have within us the seeds to do great things. Small seeds transform into large trees. The roots will tell you what type of potential this tree will grow into. Our roots are what lie within, our values and dreams. Some of us are great at telling stories. Others thrive in sport, music, inventing things or growing things.

If we did all the things we are capable of doing

we would literally astound ourselves.

Thomas Edison

Your potential is not limited. The things we do naturally point to and define our potential. The clues about what is possible for you are all around you, in your past and present. As a child, I loved to rhyme and use words. I loved to see people get excited and inspired. I dreamed of doing great things and living a great life. And those dreams and ambitions held clues about my potential. I'm still getting clues today that reveal my potential, regardless of my age. What places do you feel drawn to? What kinds of things make your heart beat faster when you think about them? What do you dream about and long to do? The world is full of opportunity!

"Looking through life I can't deny my badness,

Walk with a chip a strap I don't careless,

Fearless, I wasn't afraid to die,

Living was a mystery so don't ask me why,

In school as a youth the system fooled me,

It never schooled me as I emerged unruly,

It convinced me, I would never see my dream,

They set the limits to my future with nothing in

between,

Teachers picked on, I never picked on,

I hated lessons in this synthetic system,

Playing penny up the wall behind the shed,

Dossing in the toilet and smoking cigarettes,

When I left school with no results from exams,

I wanted a job but I couldn't get one,

The destination was set from the choices I made,

Now who's getting played?"

My goal is to see each person I inspire live their life at their optimum level. To see the fullness of their creative gifts realized, so they can live with passion and purpose, free from any limiting beliefs imposed by society or themselves! We all have untapped potential and we so often fail to embrace the best. What does our best look like and what would happen if we only accepted what was best for us instead of settling for less?

I've learned that people will forget what you said, people will forget what you did, but people will never forget how you made them feel.

Maya Angelou

> *"Now I'm a conscious youth on the verge of insanity,*
> *As I move to the street combining knowledge with reality,*
> *Trying to make a raise any way that I could,*
> *Hustling and skanking like a boy from the hood,*

> *It wasn't good, I had to open my eyes,*
>
> *Was I just another brother they would criminalise,*
>
> *Focus death another process,*
>
> *Hocus pocus street goals are all bogus,*
>
> *Hold us, unlock the mind so it will free us,*
>
> *Keep us; break the lies into pieces,*
>
> *It releases and our mentality increases,*
>
> *Death it decreases self-hate ceases,*
>
> *A broken heart is like broken glass,*
>
> *It's laying everywhere and you just can't pass,*
>
> *Your destination is set by the choices you made,*
>
> *Now who's getting played?"*

How many people do we know who have passed away never realising their potential? We need to know who we are and how celebrated we are. We all have someone cheering us on, we need to find them and allow their support to carry you. They can be hidden from sight or in plain sight. When you discover who you are, you can discern what you were made for. Only then can you find true contentment that seems so elusive. People who know their identity have nothing to prove and no one to impress. They are protected because the opinions of others hold no weight. Old coping mechanisms of comparison, envy, judgment and fear have lost their appeal. Instead, these people are pleased with who they are and unafraid of failure because their value is independent of their performance. Every decision they make and everything they do emanates from who they are! Their identity is the foundation and launch pad for their destiny.

"Don't ask yourself what the world needs. Ask yourself what makes you come alive, and go do that, because what the world needs is people who have come alive."

Howard Thurman

Pursuing our destiny is the difference between fulfilment and regret. Survive or thrive, flounder or blaze a trail, which do you choose?

We all get a significant moment to live. How will we invest our hours, days, months, years and decades? How will we make the most of all we have been given? We must align our hearts with our design so we can experience the freedom of finding our music inside!

"Amidst the whole peril in the world, here's why you're still alive–to find your purpose. Your purpose will ignite hope in others."

Chinonye J. Chidolue

Chapter 14
Finding the Music Inside

"Musicians must make music, artists must paint, poets must write if they are ultimately to be at peace with themselves. What humans can be, they must be."

Abraham Maslow

How do we inspire a generation to be their best selves? Keeping it real is a fundamental, unwritten value of true-school hip hop. Realness was always the goal; it was the ultimate claim for the successful hip hop artist. Copying and being fake, on the other hand, was the ultimate negative. Being true to oneself and representing one's place and culture were vital aspects of keeping it real. I would describe these attributes as individuality, and key to establishing your brand. It is key to developing values that allow you to build a solid foundation.

Flipping the script refers to turning the tables, doing the unexpected, or deviating from the norm. This is what makes the genre unpredictable. Hip hop as a culture is built on flipping the script, using previously existing material in new and innovative ways. From break dancers repurposing discarded flooring, to graffiti artists using trains and alleyways as canvases, to producers sampling and re-imagining previously recorded music. In the early eighties, I had access to my parents' record collection long before I was earning enough to gather my own. Hip hop has always had, at its roots, a philosophy of taking things and transforming them into something new. Hip hop artists have demonstrated creative resourcefulness with limited resources, flipping something outta nothing. In life, building adaptability into our way of working has enabled me to evolve. That is the way we turn negative thoughts into positive thoughts – the law of subtraction.

Making noise wasn't just about sound, it was the people showing love and acknowledging the art. Audiences would spark their lighters to acknowledge a song they were feeling. Sometimes you have to make noise, make those positive declarations about yourself. I can and I will.

We always wanted to stay fresh, to be original. I didn't want to be like anyone else. We developed new methods of greetings that are now commonplace. We used slang that allowed us to be different, which is now mainstream language. Today, I want this message to be fresh in all aspects of its creativity and inspire you to be all you can be.

> *We are born to bring light,*
> *Darkness descending not afraid of the night,*
> *Not afraid of the fight, wield a sword that is light,*
> *Like Tommie Smith raise a fist with the mic,*
> *Raise a fist in the light, protesting for rights,*

295

> *Wear my pants a little baggy can't wear ones that are tight,*
>
> *If you're hungry then bite, raise your chin to its height,*
>
> *Follow every crumb, insight with your sight,*
>
> *Think of every verse, every verse becomes a bar,*
>
> *Every bar becomes a phrase that you repeat in your car,*
>
> *Thinking about my lingua not just what I heard,*
>
> *Look a little deeper, legacies of every word,*
>
> *Be more than a rebel break the image of the mould,*
>
> *Change the stories that are told, I'm talking to the bold,*
>
> *For those in the struggle don't hide,*
>
> *Just play your music inside!*

Once you find your music inside, you come alive and begin to live as you were intended to live. You become what you always were in your dreams. You no longer feel the disconnect between being and doing as you align your essence on every level. It is bringing balance to your life, mind, body and soul. The purpose of music has always been to

296

communicate a message, tell a story, illustrate a drama, express emotion and thought. It has been used to heal, educate, motivate and express one's identity. It also serves the purpose of expressing one's true self. For this reason, when you find your music, it must be played, it cannot be put on the shelf. Music lifts us from our frozen mental habits and makes our minds move in ways they ordinarily cannot. Let your music play and play it loud!

We want the music inside,

Bring you something to uplift your spirit with pride,

Uplift your spirit in the night, take you high like a kite,

While I'm navigating on a dangerous flight,

No blackbox in this flight, we go under the radar,

Under the saviour releasing the vapour,

Not a crime caper, I'm reading nature,

See the signs in the sky before there blocked by

skyscrapers,

What about the future, future where creating?

> *As I release my music I am not anticipating,*
>
> *So, understand it is essential,*
>
> *When you find your music you're finding your*
>
> *potential,*
>
> *So when we play our music real loud,*
>
> *No limiting beliefs are allowed,*
>
> *For those in the struggle don't hide.*
>
> *Time to find your music inside.*

A frustrated young man went to see the wise man in his village.

"I don't know what to do with my life. How do I find my purpose?" the young man asked.

"Follow me," said the old man.

Silently, they trudged together to a faraway river where they found dozens of prospectors panning for gold.

"There are three types of prospectors here," the sage said.

"What do you mean?" the young man inquired.

298

"There are those who strike gold straight away. Excited, they take their plunder, cash it in and live comfortably for the rest of their lives. Then there are those who pan for years. They know that there is gold here and they have seen others strike it rich, so they persist until they too find the gold that they've been searching for."

"What about the third type?" asked the young man.

"They are the individuals who get frustrated that they haven't found what they are looking for, so after a day, a week or a year or more, they give up, walk away and never find gold."

Slightly confused, the young man asked, "What has this got to do with finding my purpose?"

"Aah yes, the age-old question." the old man smiled and looked his companion in the eye. "There are those in life who look for their purpose and seem to find it almost immediately. From a young age they have a clear sense of purpose and pursue their dreams with energy and enthusiasm. Some others have to look a bit harder, perhaps for many years, but if they persist and keep looking, they

299

will find something to live for. Finally, there are those who want to know their purpose, but they become frustrated with the search and give up too soon, returning to a life of meaningless wandering."

"Can everyone find their purpose?"

"Is there gold in the river?" the wise man responded.

"So, how do I find my own purpose?"

"Keep looking."

"But what if I want to find it quicker?"

"Son, there are no guarantees that you will be able to find it quickly, the only guarantee is that if you give up and stop looking for it, you'll never find it."

The young man looked despondent, feeling that he had wasted his time with the old man.

He felt a reassuring hand on his shoulder, "I can sense your frustration, but let me assure you, if you can find your true calling in life, you will live with passion, make the world a better place, be richer than you could imagine and feel as though the very face of God Himself is smiling upon you. That may happen next week, next year or in the years ahead, but the search will be worth it and your life will never be the same again. So for now, your purpose is to find your purpose."

"Thanks."

"Oh, and there's one other thing that I forgot to mention."

"What's that?"

"Just as those men and women need to get down to the river with a pan to find their gold, so we need to remain active to find our purposes, we don't find it sitting around at home doing nothing."

It was getting late, so the two men turned for home and began their long walk back to the village.

As they walked, the young man was deep in thought about what he had just learned, and the wise man smiled to himself, knowing that conversations like this were an important part of living his own purpose.

We want the music inside,

Being all you can be as you shine on this ride,

In the dark of the night, you got to be your own,

Positive thought, stay out the negative zone,

Taking every stand with intelligence is key,

I'm constructing lives like a rhyme in poetry,

You know it's me so there's no need for alarm,

I'm just releasing my music so just stay calm,

In our palms we have potential, to set this fuse alight,

With our minds in the gutter only pain will ignite,

We be able sick of all the fables,

Someone get the DJ some technics turntables,

Release the cypher, a little hyper,

Play your music, fire up those lighters,

For those in the struggle don't hide,

Just release the music inside.

When you share your music, you will live a more significant life than those who don't. I get so excited when I see someone playing their music – it doesn't matter who it is. Their freedom and joy resonate deeply within me. The greatest challenge for us is to be the person we were made to be and accept that being unique is a blessing that makes us powerful.

> *We were made to shine bright,*
> *Bring you something you can bump to in the heat of night,*
> *Born to make a difference,*
> *Raise my fist to salute with your music comes resilience,*
> *Throw your hands in the air,*
> *Wave them around like you just don't care,*
> *We make a difference worldwide,*
> *Doesn't matter where you are find the music inside.*

A sailing boat uses the power of the wind to get where it needs to go, there is a longer process involved to prepare and master, but you will always go further and, eventually, go faster than a person in a rowboat. You might have to study and become an expert, but the time taken will prepare you for the momentum shifts that are happening all the time. If you only stay with what you know, as times change, you quickly become yesterday's person. For us who have never sailed before, it easy to get into a rowboat and start rowing. You're not moving very fast but you're moving. Eventually, you can see the sailing boat catching you quickly, it goes beyond you and disappears off into the distance. By this point, you're worn out and have nothing else to give and head back to what you're familiar with.

The way the wind works, even with today's technology, is not fully understood, but the risings, failings, and change in direction many times in a day will probably always be a mystery to me. Wind is a natural movement of air in natural motion, it is similar to our music inside. It fills us with passion and purpose. In one of his poems, Wordsworth writes about a bird that was carried from Norway by a storm. It fought hard against the gale in its effort to get back to Norway. At last, it gave up fighting the wind, and instead of being carried towards its destruction, it ended up on the warm shores of England, to the green meadows and forests.

Finding our music means that our lives are lived as they were intended. We connect with our destiny. We live in harmony with our gifts and talents, utilizing each situation we face and accepting all that life throws up as part of our calling. We learn to view life with a positive outlook. Living by our music provides direction to everyday life. Yet most people today have strayed from their music and have settled for the status quo. How many people have woken up today without direction? Many others have their goals determined by what they own or earn. Our music is not an occupation a person chooses. This is career selection and we do it for financial success, security, access to power and privilege, for satisfaction and fame. The world encourages us to determine our own occupation and destiny, leaving us in conflict with our music.

- First, our music enables us to put work in its proper perspective.
- Second, our music gives us a deep sense of identity that is formed by what is inside us.
- Third, our music balances our lives, we are ready to face our successes and struggles.
- Fourth, our music exposes our motives and values by creating boundaries for what we do so that we can make a difference in the lives of others.
- Fifth, our music equips us to live with single-mindedness in the face of multiple needs and competing claims and distractions.

- Sixth, our music gives us a deep sense of integrity when living under pressures by inviting us to live against the flow of external opinion, we can never be politically correct.
- Seventh, our music helps us make sense of our lives, we can have a meaningful existence.

Live in the moment and dream big. Deny oxygen to the negative thoughts that arise from inside and out. Find the right wind, set sail, and launch out towards your dream. Your music inside is blowing, giving you the momentum you need. Be more than you feel and make the big choices as often as you can.

I have fed mouths that have talked shit about me. I've wiped tears off the faces of the people that have caused mine. I have picked up people that have tried to knock me down. I've done favors for people that can do nothing for me. I have been there for people that have not been there for me.

CRAZY? Maybe...

But I will NOT lose myself in the hatred of others; I continue to be me because I am who I am and it is my nature. Life isn't easy. but even through all the bullshit...

I will still be here, being me.

Author Unknown

I can feel myself coming in for a landing. I was an emcee and rap today is the most widely performed of the four elements of hip hop. The elements of hip hop are artistic expressions, the others being graffiti, breakdancing and DJing. The movement emerged against the odds, stirred by the civil rights movement. Jamaican DJs adapted their sound-system style of street parties to the New York ghettos, a style that meshed well with the lack of traditional facilities in abandoned neighborhoods. It was the birth of the block party. As they did so, they began to reimagine the use of vinyl records not solely as recorded music but as the raw materials for the creation of new music. These visionaries followed the music inside to create a global phenomenon. Through them this same music has reached across the Atlantic into housing estates within the UK.

As I think back and contemplate my journey, I appreciate it takes time, and a no quit mentality to see it come into fruition. From my early years I remember, my musical taste was influenced by my parents and what I saw on the radio and television. Einstein said, "A mind in motion stays in motion unless it's disturbed by an outside force." One evening, my brother Arnold decided now is the time to rescue me. He played Kurtis Blow the Breaks. He cued up the song, and I lost control of my head as it bobbed to the beat. The wordplay immediately connected with me deeply. Hearing that song, i can only describe it like eating Jerk chicken for the first time. The pounding rhythm, no compromise in style, the poetry it related connected with me. But as soon as the song finished, I made up my mind that I had to do this. Hip hop soon became my first love. It's not just the music, it is the culture that surrounds the music. I loved the fact that the melody supported by the rhythm, music prior to hip hop the rhythm supported the melody. The bass didn't play in the background, these musical pioneers brought it to the forefront, the treble had to take a back seat. For some people, this was too radical, but for me it made perfect sense. The way that every line had to rhyme with the next spoke to my love of language and poetry. The raw intensity of the music matched my own passion.

The social commentary and politics of groups like Public Enemy, Eric B and Rakim, Boogie Down Productions and NWA gave me direction and purpose. I embraced not only the music, but it enlightened me to seek and learn my own cultural backstory. This caused me to grow as a man and gave me a foundation for my future self. Before long I began writing my own rap songs, performing them on local sound systems. Wearing Symbols of Africa and quoting Malcolm X. I experienced a sense of belonging and pride. It sounds crazy to say but it felt like my eyes had been opened. For me, the world of hip hop made my world colourful and real and presented a positive reality for young men who looked like me. I felt like Dorothy landing in Oz, everything was now in high definition.

"Your vision will become clear only when you can look into your own heart. Who looks outside, dreams; who looks inside, awakens."

Carl Jung

My thought process was complicated and at times it put me at a distance from my peers and sometimes made me feel angry. Hip hop gave me an outlet and excepted me for who I was. It made me feel like I was part of something bigger than I ever could have dreamed of. It gave me a platform to be me, which led to me finding my music and performing in front of all kinds of diverse people. It was here I developed my passion for change that was imbedded in all my rhymes. It is this passion that drives me forwards and has led me to follow my music inside. Music has always been a way of me expressing myself and just like in hip hop I use it as a way to relate to others. From the biggest stages to small intimate venues I could see it in the eyes and body language of the audience as I performed. It has the power to activate the brain regions called the limbic and paralimbic areas. These areas are connected to intense reward responses, like those we experience in sex, good food and recreational drugs. For this reason, throughout history, music has been used to build and strengthen communities, and empower people.

So, what is the definition of music? Dictionary.com says; An art of sound in time that expresses ideas and emotions in significant forms through the elements of rhythm, melody, harmony, and colour. Whenever my life was out of balance, I used music as a cathartic means to give me stability. In all its nuances it made life more bearable. Artists offer us hope amid our daily struggles. Even when I faced the dark nights of the soul, certain songs carry me through, forming positive memories I can recall whenever the song is played. It provides us with a way of expressing our inner most feelings as well as our deepest emotions. Some people consider it a way to escape from the pain life tosses up, a natural endorphin. It offers us relief and allows us to reduce our levels of stress. It shows us how music plays an important role in our everyday lives more than just being a source of entertainment.

To find your music inside is to find that which is intrinsically you. That which is in you and plays quietly from your earliest moments. It nudges you towards your passion whenever opportunities arise. It evokes thoughts from my youth. Going to the record shop, searching for the imports or the illusion white labels. You always wanted a song first or the exclusive rare groove. You wanted to be the one to play something no one else was playing. As I entered the shop my excitement heightened by my expectation to find something good inside. The shop assistant would play song after song of the records freshly imported from the states. I would be patient, diligently going through each record until I found the grooves I was feeling. Once you've found it you added it to your pile you were going to purchase. In the same way you must diligently search your heart and mind. Ask yourself what made me truly happy, Find the themes. The clues to your music will always form a pattern as you look back. As a child, before the fears of adults were forced upon our subconscious, we interpreted our music inside more fluently. I always wanted to make people happy and cause young people to feel energised. I dreamed of being a voice, on stage, in print or on the street corner. But I faced a barrage of negativity, I was told to think about a real career. Being told you can't, dulls our interpretation of our music and what it means. We all need coaches, my mother always supported my music inside through encouraging words but my teachers, they said I wouldn't amount to anything. They called it a fad, if they only knew the impact of my music. It was a continual struggle, no dream is achieved without overcoming this struggle.

Within hip hop there is a term called a cipher, it comes from the word de-cipher. As in to reveal the meaning of. It was first used to mean I encode my lyrics with esoteric meaning. My rhyme was a cipher, it contains a hidden message. The Oxford Dictionary defines cypher as "a secret or disguised way of writing a code." it was used when a group of rappers, typically standing in a circle, would take turns exchanging verses together. The original meaning is like the music hidden inside of each of us that reveals our passion and purpose.

In Maslow's hierarchy of needs, our self-worth is connected to feelings of being respected. To feel valued and to know your contribution matters makes a difference to how you feel about yourself. The narrative that was pushed in the media labelled us as aggressive and violent. They portrayed us as thieves would perform at a show then do a street robbery. I know my value and within the culture we called the men kings and the ladies queens. If society won't elevate us we will elevate ourselves. After performing with Boogie Down Productions, they expressed a liking to our performance. This filled me with a sense of pride. That moment I felt the appreciation from someone I considered a hip-hop icon strengthened my resolve. This helped me build resilience in my inner world. To be respected is so important to our hierarchy of needs for this reason we see young people literally killing each other over it. I will never downplay how it feels to be disrespected and how it can evoke feelings of worthlessness. Sometimes the medicine needed is a positive word, a little encouragement, a little music. It's amazing how positive words and interactions were able to carry me towards my music. If you keep calling me great, I will rise to the challenge.

Hip hop spoke to me in a language I could understand, it sparked a fire inside of me. Now that fire communicates my truth in verse, in speech and in print. It is my belief that some thoughts and emotions can only be communicated by the energy that was birthed through hip hop. It is an energy that makes me feel alive, it is an energy that defines my music, my passion, it is me being the best me I can possibly be.

Key people at key times acted like signposts for me along the way. Lepke, Daddy Ernie, Longsey D, CJ Carlos and Edward Christie. Your character and the type of personality you have means people will either support or walk. I was privileged to have these men impact my journey, I would not have had the success I experienced without them.

Nelson Mandela, Miles Davis, DJ Kool Herc, Olajide Olayinka Olatunji known as KSI, Steve Jobs, Garrett Morgan, Thomas Edison, Rosa Parks, Greta Thunberg, Dr. Martin Luther King. They discovered their music and played it until their benefits of their music impacted those who needed it most. If you stay silent what impact could we all miss out on, we will never know. I close my eyes and I see the stage, the audience anticipating and expectant. I'm ready to be me and do what I was born to do. Fear has no place on this platform. Everyone's got that one thing they were born to do, your music inside that enables you to have more meaning in your life. It is time! Play your music inside, play it loud and be the difference the world needs.

It is time for you to draw upon your inner strength and belief. It is time you understand you are worth so much more than the status quo. Remember who you are, what your life purpose is, keep your focus and let your music inside be played on full volume. This is your time, I say this because of your genuine desire to have a great future and be free financially. Your greatest driving force and burning desire will be to give your family a great life. The only thing that can stop you from finding your Music is "you".

I have come to the understanding my success is dependent only on me. If I don't respect the moves I'm making, my dreams for my family and future, no one else will. I don't want to attract people who disrespect, distract, and weaken me from being my best self. Taking responsibility for me is choosing to live my music. I don't need your approval. My

319

experience validates my message not some other person who wants to limit my message. In the music industry they encourage you to copy what is popular. We are not designed to recreate someone else's music; our unique profile is to make our own. I refuse to live my life by the world's projection of what I am supposed to be. You get one shot at this thing called life, so be confident in every action you make. Own the consequences to your choices and grow from them all. Eminem put it best in 'Lose yourself.' *You better lose yourself in the music the moment, you own it, you better never let it go. You only get one shot, do not miss our chance to blow This opportunity comes once in a lifetime, yo.*

No more self-limiting beliefs about yourself. No more letting negative people hinder your creative prowess. No more wasting your valuable time with time wasting people and activities. You are your greatest asset, with your knowledge, experience, and all that you have been through will not only make you stronger. They have been your pathway to a greater life. The time is now, and this is your moment. Create your own destiny, if you face any unpredictable elements, stay on course and be the author of your destiny by creating your own conditions for success. This is your responsibility to yourself and your gift.

"The meaning of life is to find your gift.
The purpose of life is to give it away."
Pablo Picasso

Peace!